Love Your Body Now!

Lose The Weight Of Self-Hate

Gain The Yummy-ness Of Goddess-ness

Maria Bucaro

ISBN-13: 978-1481090964
ISBN-10: 1481090968

Dedication

I dedicate this book to *all* women, everywhere. May we walk in our beauty, right now, as we support and lift each other to the heights of all that is possible.

Author photographs by
James Scolari Photography

Titles by Maria Bucaro:

WHERE'S MY MONEY~AND ALL MY OTHER STUFF? The Ultimate
Spiritual Seekers Guide to Getting Whatever You Want

BANKRUPTCY INTO ABUNDANCE: You Guide to Prospering

LOVE YOUR BODY NOW! Lose the Weight of Self-hate
Gain the Yummy-ness of Goddess-ness

You can find more about Maria at:

www.MariaBucaro.com

Contact Maria at:

Maria@MariaBucaro.com

Acknowledgments

Clif, Shawna and Genny, Tony Robbins, Landmark Forum, Condor Vision, James Scolari Photography, Robert Scheinfeld, Deepak Chopra, Randy & Three Treasures, Ventura Center for Spiritual Living, The Fab. Four, Wayne Dyer, Access Consciousness, Human Awareness Institute and ME!

Table of Contents

Love Your Body

Now!

Introduction To Your Goddess-ness

Are you ready to love your body now and lose the heavy weight of self-hate? Yes? No? Maybe?

There is a yummy-ness in claiming the Goddess that is within you, and in order to claim the Goddess, you must first find the "groove" of what that means to you. I am not specifically talking about the airy-fairy, free flowing white dress, type of Goddess. Although that may be you. I am talking about what being in your Goddess energy means to you personally. That is your Goddess Groove. Are you ready?

When I ask this question, the response is often, "Love my body now? That's easy for you to say, and just what is it, this Goddess-ness?" I also hear "How can I love my body when there is so much wrong with it?"

When I think about getting my Goddess Groove on, I think about owning the fact that I am beautiful and sexy. Goddess Groove is all about redefining what we believe about our bodies, and knowing who we are. It is about *not* buying into what marketing and the media, our culture or others have told us to believe is beautiful.

Goddess Groove is the celebration of female sensuality and femininity. It is all about embracing and loving your beauty, both inner and outer beauty and celebrating the female form in all shapes, sizes and colors.

Your Goddess Groove is simply knowing your own God-ness and coming from that place in everything you do.

It is time to shed all of the false beliefs and critical judgments that we all have. It is time to shed the voice of negative self talk and inner self loathing. It is time to slay the beast that keeps us from living the beauty and the love and the Goddess that we are.

Love Your Body Now! is about exploring and finding out what makes you unique, both inside and out. We are all radiant, shimmering infinite beings. We are all beautiful just as we are. Did you just cringe? Somewhere you have a belief that you must look like something different than you are to be the shimmering beauty that you are. That is one big fat lie.

Our recognition of our own beauty gets hidden away because we believe the lies of what society and our culture tells us is beautiful. I say I am done with the lies. I am done trying to live up to what someone else claims is beautiful–especially because it generates money and market share (for advertising and the media) – and I claim my own definition of what is beautiful, sensuous, delicious, sexy and juicy!

Your journey through this book, as are most things in life, is a mini vision quest. As I delve deep into the art of guiding, I am seeing vision quests in every phase and part of life. The journey to loving your body is no different.

A vision quest is a rite of passage. A rite of passage is a ritual event that marks a person's transition from one status to another. By that, I mean any kind of life-changing event, from small events to really big ones. Things like puberty, birthdays, graduations, marriage, divorce, children leaving the house, a new job and even the body taking on different proportions are all considered to be rites of passage. It is a ritual death and a re-birth.

There are three components to a quest: Severance, Threshold and Incorporation. If you start to think about it, almost everything you do, especially transformational work, has these components to it.

Severance is the time of letting go of what no longer works for you. What thoughts or beliefs are you holding on to that keep you from loving your body, right now? This is the time to separate from old ways of being. What is possible for you to let go of?

Threshold is the in-between time. Think of the threshold at the door. You are neither in nor out. This is the time to learn and to play with what is coming up for you. In a vision quest, this is the time on the mountain where everything is left behind and you get to dance in the spirit world. This is where you die to the old and embrace the new. Death and re-birth. A new vision is born.

Incorporation is the time of living the new way of being. It is often said that incorporation is the most difficult of the three phases because this is where you walk your talk. Who are you now and how do you show up in the world living your new vision?

When you begin to read this book, leave behind the world as you know it, if only for the time we are together. Walk into the magic of severance and threshold time! Walk into the magic of the possibility of loving your body now, just as it is.

We will look at what you no longer want in your life. What are you walking away from? Is it other people's opinions of you? Is it your opinion of you? Is it an old belief that may not even belong to you that you have been carrying around acting as if it is your belief? Is it a voice from the past that you are still listening to? Would you like to shed the weight of self-hate?

You will have the option to let some of it go and to release old ways of being. You will have the option to envision what you want—how can you love your body right now? What would it take? What is your vision?

When you finish this book and walk in your world, how will you incorporate your new vision and new ways of being *you* into your life?

Are you ready to come out and play? Are you ready to dance with the Divine and reveal the inner truth of who you are?

I believe that one of the best ways to play and find inner beauty is through movement. The body knows how to move without anyone telling it what to do. It's about letting go and bringing forth the sensual essence that is inside just waiting to come out.

"*To love yourself as you are is a miracle, and to seek yourself is to have found yourself, for now. For now is all we have, and love is all we are.*"

—Anne Lamott

Love Your Body Now!

Can you imagine what it would feel like to love your body? Can you imagine what it would feel like to be comfortable in your own skin? Can you imagine what it would feel like to be naked with no apologies? Can you imagine what it would feel like to be comfortable without having to lose weight or to fix this or that? Comfortable because you are you and you love yourself because you are you?

I never even noticed how uncomfortable I was in my own skin until I met my husband. I thought it was normal to be all uptight about my body and to think it is not worthy to be "on display" (naked). Naked means vulnerable. For me, naked means being with the cellulite, the rolls and the saggy breasts-or being different than what I think I should look like. I'm not talking about getting naked for sex, although I'm sure that applies to some. I'm talking about looking in the mirror and loving what I see. I am talking about not hiding in a towel because I am embarrassed by how I look, but rather, glowing in who I AM.

I noticed how uncomfortable I was because my husband is so comfortable in his skin, and it showed me that I was not. When I saw how relaxed he was about his body, I knew I wanted to be like that.

I want you to know up front that I am not a medical doctor or a therapist and I do not have a degree. I am not writing this to share research and data with you. I am writing this to share my life experience with you and to let you know that it is possible, even though you don't believe it right now, to be comfortable in your own skin and to love your body, no matter what you *think* you look like! I am writing this with the hope that something will trigger in you to walk through the portal of a direct experience of *Truth*. My desire for you is to have a direct experience of knowing the infinite, beautiful being that you are.

Change and transformation does not happen in your head. It does not happen because you read a book, study a course in _____, go to a seminar or because someone else tells you "how" to transform old ways of being. Transformation happens when you move out of your head and out of "logic" and into the land of feelings. Transformation happens at the heart level and it can happen in a heartbeat. It does not happen by thinking it through logically (which is different than using your thoughts to create).

As I tell some of my stories, look and see through the lens of your own life. What stories do you have that have kept you in the place of "not enough"?

Transformation happens when you open up to the possibility of transformation and the possibility of a *direct experience*. A direct experience is just that-an experience that you have yourself. It is something that you feel, rather than something that you think. Your body knows when it feels *truth*, and when you have this experience something changes within you. I give examples of direct experiences that I have had throughout this book.

When you question what else is possible, new ways of being present themselves and this is what you can step into. Step into the true joy that you are; the beauty and the Goddess that you are *right now*!

"You are not a mistake. You are not a problem to be solved. But you won't discover this until you are willing to stop banging your head against the wall of shaming and caging and fearing yourself."

—Geneen Roth

Distorted Body Image

Body image refers to how you see your body when you look into a mirror and how you feel about your body regarding your beauty and attractiveness. A distorted body image is when the image you have in your mind is not congruent with reality—how other people see you.

Please note that I am not referring to body dysmorphic disorder. BDD is a condition that involves obsessions, which are distressing thoughts that repeatedly intrude into a person's awareness. With BDD, the distressing thoughts are about perceived appearance flaws to the point of believing that he/she is too ugly or disfigured to be seen.

Do you feel uncomfortable in your skin? Is there something about your body that makes you crazy? I am not just referring to just the "f" word (fat), although that is probably the most common distorted body image issue. I am referring to any part of your body that you are not comfortable with. It could be your nose. In a recent workshop a woman had what is referred to as a hawk nose, and is considered to be unattractive because it has a large profile. She was obsessed with her nose. Because of her nose nothing was right with her body. She could never be thin enough, muscular enough or beautiful enough to make up for her nose.

It could be the size and shape of toes, the shape of the eyes, breast size, skin color or hair texture. In my workshops, women talk about their body image and the pain that it brings them. I am no longer surprised at the power something like toes can have over someone's life. All of the parts of the body can be seen with a distorted body image. It doesn't matter what part of the body it is-if it causes you pain, then it is painful.

What is it for you? When did it start for you?

For me, I think it started when I developed breasts. This happened to me before anyone else in my class. I was only ten. This was so embarrassing to me because we wore school uniforms that made it worse. The top was a V that came from the shoulder to the waist and it totally accentuated the chest. Everyone's was flat, except for mine.

I wore sweaters in the soaring heat, hoping to hide and disguise something I had no idea what to do with. I was laughed at and ridiculed by boys and girls alike. I felt shame about my body. I did not understand what my body was doing, or why I looked different than every other girl my age. I had no friends because I saw myself as a freak and I believed everyone else saw me that way too. My breasts caused me a lot of pain because I did not understand and because I was so different.

During the next few years, more girls started to develop and I felt a little more *normal*, whatever that is. The school uniform changed in Junior High: the top was a vest, and I could take off the sweaters and not feel like the eyes of the world were upon me, laughing. I began to fit in.

Life was better and I was coming into my own. I was somewhat happy with who I was becoming and I was getting ready for what I thought was the most important moment in life-becoming a teenager! I found a group of friends that I was comfortable with and they were comfortable with me. At least I thought so. I knew that I wasn't the "popular" girl, but for some reason, one of the popular girls befriended me and I got to hang out with them-on occasion.

I turned thirteen and I was in the eighth grade. Life was going okay, I felt like I was pretty cool and the world was open and waiting for me! My breasts were no longer a big issue, although they were pretty big. I still felt some shame about them because I knew that the boys liked big breasts, and I didn't really know what that meant. I thought it was a good idea to hide them as much as possible. The good news was "those girls" did not rule my life. I was happy.

Just when I was starting to feel okay about my body, I got *slammed.* I was sitting in a car with a group of my friends. It was after school and we were being driven home by one of the moms. She had big news and we were excited to hear it. She told us that there was going to be a fashion show at our school, and she thought one of us would be perfect to be in the fashion show as a model.

As I was growing up, I was always told that I should be a model. Not because of my "beauty," but because I had the body for it. I was tall, had long legs and was very thin. I heard it a lot from my family. "Oh, you are so thin and tall, you should be a model". And I believed it. It wasn't so much that I wanted to be a model, but I really believed that I could be because of what I was told by my family. In my mind, models were "special" and who doesn't want to be special?

When my friend's mom said that one of us would be a perfect model for the fashion show, I *knew* it was me. I said with all of the conviction of a new teen, "That's me! I'd love to do it." I will never forget the look on her face. She was driving and she turned around to look at me in disbelief. Then she sneered. Then she laughed. Then she asked me if I was kidding. Then everyone laughed. Everyone was laughing at me. They all thought I was joking or more like I was a joke.

If I could have disappeared into the cracks of that back seat and gone into oblivion, I would have, never to be seen again.

This mom went on to tell us who would be the perfect model-of course it was the most popular girl, the red head that all of the guys were crazy about.

In that moment everything changed about how I saw myself. I had believed what others told me in a positive way, and in an instant, all of that went away. I knew they had lied to me. I was not model material. I was not tall and thin and I did not have long legs. I was fat. And certainly not pretty. I was just the girl that got to tag along with the popular, pretty and thin kids. This was the beginning of my Distorted Body Image.

That moment in time changed the way I heard compliments. I heard them as lies. Not only did I perceive my body in a negative way, when people said complimentary things to me, I heard them as lies. And when people said negative things about me, I believed that to be true. Why would I believe the bad, and not believe the good? Because somewhere deep inside I knew that I wasn't enough.

I grew up believing what others, outside of my family, thought about me was true and since others didn't think much about how I looked, I didn't think much about how I looked and it stopped me cold from doing something that I loved to do.

I found that I had a passion for dance. In high school there was a dance club called Orchesis. In my school, being a member of Orchesis was even cooler than being a cheerleader. We taught classes and did performances. When I danced, I was on a high like no other. I loved to choreograph dances as well as dance. One night after a particularly wonderful and fun performance, my boyfriend came up to me and I was expecting him to tell me how amazing I was and how much he enjoyed my performance. Instead he told me that I was a complete embarrassment to him and that I should never, ever, move my body that way in front of other people. In that moment, I felt shame. Because I gave so much power to other people, especially him, I stopped dancing.

As time went on, other people's thoughts and ideas ruled the way I lived. I did not believe in myself. I trusted what other people thought and said. I began to believe that these thoughts were my thoughts. I believed I was an embarrassment. Even though I was not conscious about this, these thoughts were powerful and they became my belief system. Every time I would look in a mirror, I would disrespect myself in my thoughts. Every time I would be walking down the street and see myself in a store window, I would disrespect myself in my thoughts. More Distorted Body Image.

Even as an adult, these beliefs ran my life. I became very conscious of how I looked and was always trying to be thinner. I was never enough and I was never happy with how I looked. Every time I saw a picture of myself or looked at myself in the mirror, I did not like what I saw. I wanted to change myself and look different. It didn't matter what the scale said, because it could always be less.

I remember being 18 years old and weighing 118 pounds. I was 5' 5" and I thought that I was too heavy. It wasn't until I was 57 years old that I saw the insanity of thinking I was too heavy. Distorted Body Image.

Is anything coming up for you? Are you getting the idea that other people have put ideas and thoughts into your head, and you took the ideas to be yours, and believed them, no matter how crazy they sounded? Most of us, at some point in our lives, started to believe false thoughts about our bodies. Where did you get your thoughts and ideas of your body image?

The upside of walking through the pain!

Yes, we all have body image issues. Getting your Goddess Groove on is about moving forward and using what you have learned to help not only yourself but others. How can you influence someone else by having walked through your pain and into your Goddess-ness?

Having gone through the pain of having breasts when no other girls did, or thinking I was beautiful when, clearly others didn't, I did not want my daughters to suffer the same pain. I know we can't keep them safe from everything, but I did do my best to encourage a positive body image. Here is a note from my daughter when I asked her about one of her defining moments in her life:

"One of the most defining moments of my life happened in a locker room in the fourth grade. I was on a class field trip, with my momma along as a chaperone for the weekend. All of the girls had to shower in a communal bathroom, which offered very little in the way of privacy. This was somewhat alarming to most of the pre-pubescent girls, myself included. After a hurried rinse off, I scuttled back to the dressing area to don my clothing as quickly as humanly possible. In the middle of my frantic redressing, my mom interrupted me, and pointed at one of my classmates. Carry was one of those "early bloomers," tall, and well on her way to ownership of a pair of fabulous breasts. She didn't just walk out of the shower room; she strutted, displaying with pride her freshly cleaned birthday suit. In this moment of shock of and awe, my momma whispered to me, "See that, Shawna? THAT is how you should carry yourself."

My momma later explained to me the pain of getting breasts before any of her classmates, and how, out of embarrassment, she would try to hide them with baggy clothing and hunched shoulders. She told me that she was wrong to feel shame in her body, and that I must always be proud of myself, in my own skin. This stuck with me because my boobies were not long behind Carry's. As my body developed, it did not shape into what many people would consider "perfect". I am 5'2", and no means "skinny". I do however have a rock'n bod, by MY standards. I don't care about anyone else's. In that locker room, I learned that the only thing that matters is having the confidence to be who and what you are. So the heck what if it's different from what everyone else has?! Be YOU, and strut it!"

I was able to say this to her at the time, but I was still struggling with my own body image. I could see it from the outside and I could help her, but I was unable to fully step into my own. That would come later!

"Listen to the wisdom of your body. Move the body's way Your body knows. This is where your power lies..."

—Kate Nash

Can We Be Kind To Our Bodies?

Much of my transformation began when I did a mastery program which was put on by a very big name in the transformation industry. It was an incredible experience and came at a time in my life where transformation was not only wanted but very much needed.

I learned a lot about myself, and I also began to see what worked for me and what did not work for me. At one of his events he talked about our body image and specifically losing weight. At the time, I had him on a pedestal and believed anything he said. I put more significance on things that he said and totally did not have my own "mind." How often do we do that? Just because someone is an expert or is making a lot of money touting their message does not mean it is true, and, more important, true for us. Maybe it is true for them, but we don't have to take it as our own. This is also true for anything that I say. Feel it in your body, and if it feels light, then you are on to knowing your truth. If it feels heavy, you are uncovering a lie. If what I am saying feels untrue for *you,* discard it and move on.

At the time, when he talked about body image and what to do if we wanted to lose weight, I totally bought into what he was saying. And the most insidious part of it was that it fed into what I already believed.

Now, many years later, I have to respectfully disagree with him on this one. He said that if we wanted to lose weight and really be successful at it, we need to speak the truth about how we looked. He said we need to look into the mirror and say what is true. Calling a spade a spade, if you will. The idea was to be honest with yourself about how you look and that is where your power for change resides. The exercise we were to do was to look in a mirror each day, and if you think you have a big butt, you need to look in the mirror and say: "I have a huge butt. Or what about your thighs—what awful fat thighs I have. Or look at that gut—could it get any fatter?"

I understand what he is trying to say and I disagree. I disagree because we don't really know what we look like. Remember the distorted body image? I thought I was fat weighing 118 pounds. And even if we do want to lose weight, being unkind and waging war on our bodies is not a way to be successful.

I disagree because when we are mean and call ourselves names, we are not living the truth of who we really are. Would we ever say that to anyone else?

I disagree because when we disrespect our bodies by calling it names and hating what our body is, we are simply calling into our being more of what we hate. Think about the law of attraction.

Simply put, the law of attraction states that you attract into your life that which you think about. If you are constantly thinking about how awful your body is, your body is awful. If you are constantly saying that you have a big butt, you have a big butt. Your thoughts create the life you have, right now. This applies to *everything* in your life, including how you see and feel about your body.

Assuming responsibility for your thoughts is really important. If you want to see beauty in yourself, see beauty in everything and everyone. If you want to have peace in your life, see peace in everything and everyone. If you want to have love in your life, then see love for everyone and everything. If you want kindness in your life, be kind to everyone—yourself included!

If you keep looking in the mirror and tell yourself that you are ugly, fat, too thin or whatever, you will continue creating the same problems just by noticing them. Saying it out loud and carrying those thoughts with you throughout the day totally locks in that reality. You will do things that support that reality.

If every time I look into a mirror I am putting myself down and looking at the fat and hating it, I am calling in more of that. I am stuck in the endless rut of always thinking about what I don't like. I am stuck in the endless rut of dieting and working out. And it does not work.

For me, the part I have not liked in the past is my stomach. I have always had the idea that a flat stomach is sexy and attractive. And why wouldn't I think that? You don't see models in magazines or movie stars in movies having rounded tummies. Everyone is thin, has flat stomachs and wears a size 0. And from there, the airbrushing begins! How real is that? And really, how attractive is that? What about hair? Seriously, not many of us are blessed with long, thick luxurious hair. When we set that as our standard of what is beautiful or what a Goddess is, most of us will come up seriously lacking. Wow, that feels really heavy.

I needed to change my thoughts on what I consider sexy. Not my partner's thoughts, not the media's thoughts; my thoughts. Because here is the good news. When you assume 100% responsibility for everything you are experiencing in your reality, in your life right now, accepting that your thoughts create your reality, then *you* have the power to alter your reality by changing your thoughts.

Your world is your creation. Feel amazed by that! Find the beauty in your world and feel grateful for that beauty. If you want to see yourself differently, then consciously begin to see yourself as you want to be. Start to dwell on your beauty. Start to see what is beautiful right now. Begin creating the beauty you truly want by holding the intention of beauty.

Do you want to feel sexy? You don't need to wait for something to happen. Be sexy now. You don't have to be Marilyn Monroe–be who you are and be what you define as sexy. Is that too big of a move for you? Then do it in baby steps. If you are feeling frumpy, what is the next thing you can feel on the way to sexy? Maybe the only thing you need to do is put a smile on your face.

Think about what you desire, and no longer think about what you don't want. What is your heart's desire? The easiest way to do this is to pay attention to your emotions. Thinking about your heart's desires feels good, and thinking about what you don't want feels bad. What feels light? If it feels heavy, and you notice yourself feeling bad, you've caught yourself thinking about something you don't want. Now simply see what you want as already done. How does it feel?

This sounds really simple, right? It is. Maybe that's why we don't do it on a regular basis. This is no big secret and it's not hard. Our stories make it seem difficult and challenging. Get rid of the stories and move on to feeling good!

When you focus toward what you do want, your emotional state will improve really quickly. As you do this repeatedly, you'll begin to see your physical reality shift too, first in subtle ways and then in much bigger ways.

I believe we need to be kind and gentle to ourselves. When we are kind to ourselves, we open up to receiving kindness from others. Let me say that again-when we are kind to ourselves, we open up to receiving kindness from others. The same thing applies to love. When we love ourselves, we open up to receiving love from others. How can we possibly receive love from someone when we don't receive it from ourselves?

I believe that we need to love the parts that we don't particularly like. It's time to make friends with the rolls and the scars and the cellulite and the sags. It's time to make friends with thinning hair, large noses, large/small breasts and things that jiggle! It's time to jiggle the jiggle and laugh with joy. Why? Because it's your body and you're alive and all you have is this moment. Are you willing to give up this beautiful moment in your life because you want to stay stuck in the "yuck"? Or are you willing to get over it? Are you willing to get over the stories you tell yourself and start to love yourself?

Getting your Goddess Groove on is about joy and laughter. It is about lightening up and knowing that you are so much more than the jiggle. The scars tell a story. The wrinkles tell a story. You are a wonder simply because you are here. Love the moment, love yourself and love your body.

When I talk about loving your body now and getting over it, I am often asked "does that mean I shouldn't take care of myself and exercise or color my hair if I don't want the gray or can I eat anything I want?" I am not saying that we should not take care of ourselves. It is just the opposite. When we love our bodies and we can be friends with it, we want to take care of it. It is no longer a chore or hardship. It is a natural way of being.

There is nothing wrong with wanting to look your best. The problems come from thinking that if you look good, then you are worthy. This idea of self-worth comes from many places. It can come from childhood and how you were treated by your parents. It can be self-imposed. For me, it came from my ex-husband. We would go out every Friday for date night. I would need to get "dressed up" to go out, which meant I needed to look fantastic and sexy. Then, if I looked "good enough," I could order champagne and have a very expensive dinner as a reward. My worth was all tied up with how I looked, and I bought into it for many reasons, which aren't important to go into. Ultimately it was my responsibility to say "no more." In finally saying no more, I was practicing kindness to myself.

Kindness in Eating

You can also practice kindness to yourself when you eat. You do not need to be at war with yourself every time you eat. Eating nourishes your body and it is about nourishing your soul. Eating is not about restriction and "not having." It is not about denial and deprivation. When we deny and deprive ourselves we are certainly in a losing game. And we are not losing weight!

We want to eat foods that leave us feeling full of energy and light. We want to eat foods that nourish our souls as well as our bodies. We want to be light and move with grace and ease. And we want that food to be really yummy, you know, actually taste good!

When I eat something that is really yummy (my Mom's spaghetti and meatballs!) and I have *perceived* that it is not good for me (carbs and red meat), I don't enjoy what I am eating. So what's the point of eating it? What I have learned is to eat that plate of spaghetti and meatballs and savor it and enjoy it. It is no longer the forbidden fruit-it is just another choice. I don't want to waste time beating myself up about it or feeling guilty.

As you honor your body and are kind to it you will ultimately, over time, desire that which feeds you physically and emotionally. Your body will crave foods that nourish you in all ways.

We always have a choice about what we do, how we do it and when we do it. There is no judgment about different types of food, amounts of food or how often one eats. Nothing is good or bad, right or wrong. It simply is. Let your body be your guide. Your body knows.

Your body knows what it wants. Sometimes a simple question to the body will help you. Ask your body what it wants. Let's say that you would like a nice hunk of crispy, crunchy bread. Have a piece of bread. Often after piece I will automatically go for another. There is nothing right or wrong about having another piece of bread. My body may or may not want it. So I can ask—"body, would you like another piece of bread?" Then I go with the answer. You can apply this to everything that you put into your body.

I am not a nutritionist and I am not giving advice on what to eat or what not to eat. If you are unsure of what your body wants, experiment and see how you feel after eating certain things. Your body may not like gluten. Your body may not like red meat. Your body may love veggies and chocolate! The key here is to listen to your body and honor what it wants.

Kindness in Movement

We are here to express ourselves freely and energetically with movement and feeling. When we come from the feeling of self/body expression as the infinite being that we are, it becomes a natural way of being to move and express.

Be gentle and kind to yourself. Getting your Goddess Groove on is about being kind to yourself. Your inner Goddess wants you to treat yourself like you would treat your best friend. It is not about punishing yourself with physical exercise for the sake of losing weight. It is not about lifting weights and suffering. And there is nothing wrong with lifting weights or going out for a run! It is about doing what feels good and is joyful. It is all about movement and self expression. It is about being in your body and enjoying all of the things your body can do! What type of movement feels amazing and fun to you? Do that!

What I love to do is swim and dance and ride my bike. Sometimes I like to lift weights.

There is a beautiful outdoor pool that I go to with a friend. When we go together, it becomes a time of meditation. I am immersed in the joy of swimming. It is a time of stretching, breathing and praying. We also love stopping along the way to chat. How does it get any better than that?

Dancing Nia, with Kate Nash at Cosmotion in Ventura, has opened my life to amazing possibilities. I am free to be me, to dance like no one is watching along with a community of beautiful, free, open, non-judgmental spirits. I am filled with joy and I sweat like crazy! I don't consider it "working out," and it is the best work out I've ever had! If you can find somewhere to go and dance with other Goddesses, do it now! Being around others who love to move is inspiring and you also get to see other women, with all different shapes and sizes, loving themselves and being free to be.

I love to ride my bike as my mode of transportation whenever I can. It feels great, it's green and riding keeps me toned. I don't do it because it keeps me toned or because it's green. I do it because I feel great when I ride my bike. In fact, I feel young and I feel cool. And it makes me smile. I put on music that I love and go into meditation and prayer; however I do need to stay present with traffic!

Explore and find out what you love to do. Is it dancing, walking, hiking, swimming, bike riding, gardening, climbing trees—what is juicy for you? When you do what turns you on and lights you up, it won't be a chore. Do it *now!* Don't wait to lose weight, buy that cute outfit or put it off until you have enough energy. Create your life as you want to live it. You will be expressing yourself as the Goddess you are. Find your groove and go and you will experience the yummy-ness of Goddess-ness!

I believe that when we are kind to our bodies, when we love our bodies, just as we are, we honor the physical form that we came here to play with. When we honor our bodies, we will keep them healthy and fit without having to "work out" in painful ways or deprive and starve ourselves.

Self-Esteem And Body Esteem

Self-esteem and body esteem are two different things. Self-esteem is the big picture-how we think about ourselves in our relationships, how we do our jobs, how we live our values, what we have accomplished in our lives. It is all about how we feel about ourselves in general.

Do we love fully? Are we kind? Do we contribute to the world we live in? Are we happy? In other words, it is a measure of how we are generally doing in life.

Body esteem is all about how we think and feel about our bodies. Do we judge our bodies to be too thin, too fat, nose too big, not enough hair, too much hair, too tall, too short?

Body esteem is a part of self-esteem; however, we often look to our body esteem to judge how our lives are going and how we feel about ourselves.

If we have poor body esteem, a negative body image, we cannot feel good about anything that we do. All of our accomplishments go out the door if we put on a few extra pounds. All of the great acts of contribution and kindness that we do have no meaning if we don't feel good about how we look. Does this sound familiar?

When we are disrespecting ourselves in the mirror, we are not honoring who we are. Our life is only meaningful if we look acceptable to other people. If we have poor body esteem, then we have poor self esteem, no matter how fantastic we are in other ways. Wow! How does that feel? Is that true?

Here are the questions that I have: Who gets to decide what is beautiful? Who gets to decide what is pleasant to look at? Who gets to decide what is perfect for us? Who gets to decide what needs to be changed and if changed, into what? Who gets to decide if what I see when I look in the mirror is good enough?

I have been on a spiritual quest for the past 13 years. In that quest I have questioned what I am about, who I am and what is the Truth with a capital T.

On my quest I have discovered some Truths. One of the Truths, actually what I consider to be *The Truth*, is that we are all connected, all One. This is not new information. This is ancient wisdom which can be dated back to Greek Philosophers before the Bible was even written.

What that means to me is that, I am and you are, One with Source. Source, Spirit, God, Universe, Higher Power, Infinite Being-whatever you want to call it, it is all the same. It is that feeling and knowing that lives deep inside of us and flows through each and every one of us. It is a knowing that there is so much more of who we are and we can't see it, but we know. It is a knowing that we are not just this body and that each of us is connected.

I believe that Spirit flows through me and Spirit flows through you. Does that mean we are Divine? Yes! That means that I am Divine and you are Divine. You may have heard someone say "Namaste." The simple definition of Namaste means, the Divine in me, seeing the Divine in you.

How can I really believe this if I am looking at myself and judging that I am not good enough? That my body is not good enough? That I see myself though the judgmental eyes of others?

How can I really believe this if I am looking at you and judging that you are not good enough? That your body is not good enough?

Who gets to decide what is good enough? Or what beautiful enough is?

I have been, and still am, on a quest to find how I can live congruently with my spiritual beliefs, and how I see and feel about myself. It has been said, that when I disrespect myself, that is a form of blasphemy. When I don't honor the truth of who I am, and I put myself down, I am also disrespecting the God in me. How often do you disrespect yourself?

I am a vision quest Guide and where I really hear and see and learn is in nature. Nature is a beautiful mirror that reflects beauty in abundance! I am at home in nature, love to be in nature and feel most alive when I am in the mountains or walking the beach.

And when I am in the mountains or on the beach I am still judging myself and the way that I look. Hmm . . .

I know that my work is to be congruent with my beliefs. I have tried all of the tips-look in the mirror and find some part of my body that I love, stare into my eyes and recite affirmations, etc. Nothing I tried worked for me for the long term. That may be true for you also.

After trying one exercise after another, I would still look at my reflection in a store window and go "yuck." Sometimes it would be out loud, other times that voice inside my head would shout out *"yuck."* I would put on an outfit and stand in the mirror and suck in my stomach and wish it to be different. *Really, really* wish it to be different. In my mind, if I could look thin (flat stomach to be exact) I would be worthy. Worthy of what? Worthy of love, worthy of kindness, worthy of money, worthy of friendship.

My very best friend lives out of state. When I was living in this insanity, I would make sure that when I saw her, I would be thinner. I would diet, exercise and do my best to look my best. Part of it was to be worthy of her friendship. But the nasty part, the shadow part that I am not proud of, was to be better than her. In elementary school and in high school she was always "the pretty one." I always held her to be the beautiful one and I was just her side kick. There was a part of me that wanted to be "more" and better than her—tanner, thinner, sexier. I think it really came down to wanting to prove that I was worthy of her friendship. I was operating and creating this friendship with really poor body esteem.

Poor body esteem can wreak havoc on intimate relationships. For me, walking around naked was out of the question. Remember in the beginning of this book, I talked about my husband being so comfortable walking around naked. He loves me to be naked too. But the cellulite, the rolls, the wrinkles, the saggy breasts pointing south. Oh—my-gosh—there was no way!

My journey with my body image went into high gear when I went to a workshop nine years ago. The name of the workshop was Love, Intimacy and Sexuality. I went to fix myself because I believed I was flawed when it came to love and sexuality. (This is a whole different book!) I had no idea what I was in for.

At the time I was living in Colorado and the workshop was in Northern California. I remember calling my mom from the airport in Denver, telling her I was going to this workshop. She said something about those "Northern Californians" being weird, and I laughed. I did not really understand what she was talking about. I went to the workshop with an open mind and I was willing to learn new things.

It all started out pretty cool on Friday night, and into Saturday morning. As we were sitting in small groups, during a closed-eye process the facilitator said that this was now the time of the workshop to take off our clothes, if we wanted. It wasn't mandatory, it was optional. Of course I thought she was kidding. Who in the world would take off their clothes in the middle of a workshop with a whole bunch of people around? But as I sat there with my eyes closed, I heard this rustling, which sounded a lot like people taking off their clothes. No way. Who would do that? Well, apparently about 70 people would do that.

When I opened my eyes, there were a lot of naked people standing around. I, of course, still had my clothes on. There were a few of us who still did. We gathered into a circle and were told to look at each other and take in all of the different shapes and sizes. The old, the young, the heavy, and the thin and everything in between. There were people of all different ages and shapes and sizes!

As I stood there, looking around the room, I became really uncomfortable. I could not look at anyone. I burst into tears and needed to leave the room. I fled. I couldn't breathe. It wasn't about naked people and being offended by nakedness. It wasn't even about it being weird. I just couldn't look at them. I developed a knot in my stomach that felt like a tree root—all gnarly and nasty, and the nasty, tight feeling just grew and grew.

I wanted to leave, but because I had someone pick me up at the airport and drive me there, I had no way to leave. That was all I wanted to do. I wanted to get out of there and fast. I could go and camp out in the woods until the workshop was over and then leave—except it was pouring rain and I had no tent. There was no alternative but to stay. I decided I could stay but not go back into the room where the workshop was being held. I could stay and not talk to anyone else, but just hide away in a corner until it was over and then get out of this place.

Facilitators of the workshop came out to see if they could help me. They tried talking and working with me but they could not reach me, or find out what was going on with me.

As the day progressed, it just kept getting worse. Finally, at midnight it came to me. I realized that all of those naked people were totally vulnerable standing there. I knew that there was no way I could stand naked, because there was no way I could be vulnerable. Not to them, not to anyone. I had to be strong and protect myself. It was the first time I realized that I did not let people in. I was not intimate with people because I needed to protect myself from being hurt.

I really want to say this again because it is one of the biggest keys to intimacy and happiness. *Vulnerability.* I could not be present in the room because I could not be vulnerable. Are you vulnerable? What does that mean? To me, at that time, it meant that if they could see me, I mean really see me, they would not like me. They would know that I am not enough. And so I put up walls of being superior, aloof, cold and out of reach. This creates separation and is so sad not only for me but for everyone around me.

On the final day, I was able to go back into the room, and that was the beginning of my process to open myself up and to let people in. I have always been invisible, and I realized it was time for me to start to become visible. I did keep my clothes on, and I was able to start to participate in the workshop.

The journey since then has taken me to an awakening of who I am, finding my juiciness and passion and living into it. I discovered vision questing and found it to be such a profound experience that I became a Guide because I wanted to be able to share this rich gift.

Getting your yummy Goddess Groove on is all about being juicy, passionate and vulnerable. Then, coming from this place, giving your gift.

Whose Idea Is It?

Ever since I was ten years old, developed breasts and had my "lady days," I have known that I was unattractive and kind of a freak. Then with the "model" experience that I talked about earlier, I really believed and thought of my body as being unattractive. Like I said, I was 18, weighed 118 pounds and did not like the way I looked. I know that it has nothing to do with how I look, but how I *think* I look.

Beauty and body image is total perception. Think back to the Renaissance period where it was beautiful to be full bodied. It is the social consciousness that determines what is beautiful. Why am I showing you this picture? Because it is only beautiful because as a whole,  society decided it was beautiful. When we look at pictures from this period, we see women who have some meat on their skin. It was deemed attractive and sexy then. Now, this woman would be considered to be a plus size and not exactly the standard of beauty. (Although I personally disagree and find her to be quite beautiful).

The point I want to make is beauty is defined by others, and we buy into it. Our bodies are not designed to be a size zero. Why do we make war on our bodies to meet someone else's standards? Why do we work so hard for something that is unattainable? Why do we know the models in magazines do not look like that in real life and yet we *still* try to look like that?

Think about tribal Africa and what is considered to be beautiful in that faraway, beautiful place. Large holes in the earlobes, as well as in the lips. Would you consider these holes to be beautiful in your world? And yet it is considered to be beautiful there. We are always choosing what is beautiful.

The really good news is we can change our thoughts about what we believe is beautiful. We can determine what is beautiful for us. Yes, maybe it is holes in our ears, or thin and not plump, or plump and not thin. We get to decide for ourselves what is beautiful!

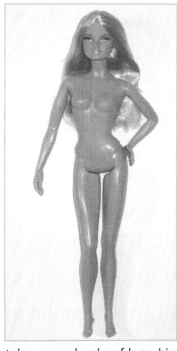

Where did it come from that we need to be thin to be beautiful? We grew up with dolls that relayed what beauty is supposed to be to us. Even though it is impossible to look like Barbie, this is the image that taught us what beauty is.

Of course, there are the magazine ads that we are bombarded with that tell us what beauty is. And here is the kicker. Even knowing that no one really looks like that, we still strive to look like that. And we think less of ourselves if we don't look like that. Even knowing that all of the ads are airbrushed to take away wrinkles and lines, airbrushed to take away chunks of legs, hips and stomach to make the model appear to be thinner-even knowing that, we still think less of ourselves because we don't measure up and look like that.

Why? Damned if I know. You thought I was going to have some great

Your beauty is defined by you!

answer, right? I really don't know. And I am done trying to figure it out. I am done with being not enough, and separate from who I am. I am done with not being happy in my body, and I am *really* done with someone else telling me what I am and am not. I am done with not loving me because someone else has other ideas as to what is beautiful. I am done trying to look like someone that I am not. I am done thinking that the only way to be sexy and wanted is to have a flat stomach along with long, straight thick hair. I am done.

What is important is that we stop buying into the marketing schemes that assault us on every level. We must stop the insanity of believing that if we purchase that car, we will look like "they" do. Even worse, if we purchase that car we will be happy. We must stop the insanity of buying into "thin is beautiful." We must stop the insanity of thinking "if I could only look like "her," my life would be great!" We must stop the insanity of buying products that don't work, but give the promise of looking younger-as if that is what life is about! I am done letting the advertisers rule what I think is beautiful and fun and sexy. I am done.

I realize that I am not going to change the billion dollar business of marketing over night, if at all. Of course, I would like to see more companies creating marketing campaigns that speak to women as real women. I would love to see more TV characters that look like real women look. It may happen at some point, but I don't see it happening any time soon. That means it is up to me to determine what I think, and not buy into some male executive's idea of what I should look like, or aspire to. And maybe, just maybe by all of us standing in our Truth of what is beautiful we will change the way business and marketing is done in the future, for our daughter's daughters.

Getting my yummy Goddess Groove on means that I define what is beautiful. My beauty is defined by me. I am beautiful.

If you are wondering how I got to this place, I explain it a little later.

"We survey lush landscapes with variations not dissimilar to a so-called "imperfect" female body with absolute pleasure -- say, an expanse of Irish countryside with grassy rolling hills. But is it really so much uglier when it's made of flesh instead of soil?"

— Kim Brittingham

Phenomenal Woman

What would it take to be a phenomenal woman? Do you want to change your definition of what a phenomenal woman is-what a Goddess is? Do you understand that by changing how you think, it changes how the world thinks?

This is really true! Just as media and advertising influence and change the way we think about ourselves, it can go the other way also. There is a tipping point, and as we stand together in defining our own unique beauty, we can change how our culture thinks about beauty.

Not only is this important from a "global" point of view, it is really important from our personal point of view. I am referring to how others in our own lives treat us and see us. When we stand in the power of knowing our own bodies and defining our own beauty on *our* terms we change the way others see us.

I was having a conversation with Clif, my husband, about this the other day. He was talking about what my owning what is sexy and beautiful means to him. My sexiness has nothing to do with my weight or what I am wearing. My sexiness is all about how I stand in knowing my sexiness. If I am worried about a roll or cellulite or the fact that I perceive my boobs to be too big, he will pick up on the energy and I won't be very attractive to him, or to myself. If I love my body, now, no matter where it is at in weight or breast size, that is the energy that I will be putting out. Loving my own body is very attractive to him. I am open and light and a whole lot more fun! That is very attractive to him. And he says that is attractive to other men as well.

Granted, there are some men who are only after the "Playboy" type, or can only be attracted to someone who is a nine or a ten (and by whose measurement anyway?) but my question is, "Is that someone you want in your life?" Too often we as women believe that we should/must look perfect to be attractive. The truth is our attractiveness lies in the mind. Our own mind. When we think we are not enough, then we are not enough. When we think we are not beautiful, juicy, sexy Goddesses, then we are not all of that.

If that is true, then how cool is it that if we believe we *are* beautiful, juicy, sexy Goddesses, then we are all of that? Oh, Yes! If you don't believe me, try it out for a week and see what happens. Each time you start to think that you are not "all of that," change your thoughts to thinking you are. Walk it, talk it, feel it and be it. You are all of that!

Transforming how the world thinks and defines beauty may also include opening the eyes of how your partner sees you and defines beauty. Transformation starts with each individual. I know that for myself, I spent many years having my beauty and my sexiness defined by my partner. It was what turned him on that I became, and it had nothing to do with me or what turned me on. In fact, I had no idea what my own definition of sexy was, let alone how to be the Goddess that I am.

The reason I allowed him so much power over me was because I thought that I was not good enough. If I dressed in a way that I felt was attractive and he told me I wasn't attractive, that reinforced that I wasn't enough. If I gained a few pounds and he made comments about it, that reinforced that I wasn't enough. If he couldn't get sexually turned on because of how I looked, that reinforced that I wasn't enough. If I walked around in an old comfy bathrobe, and he told me I was "frumpy" that reinforced that I wasn't enough.

The truth is, it was my responsibility to stand up and say *"No more!* You cannot criticize my body or me." By feeling shame and unworthiness, I allowed him to continue to bully me. It is my responsibility to say "This is who I am, the woman you married, the mother of our children, the partner that shares your life. I am a Goddess, I am funny, I am sexy, I am valuable, I am lovable, I am smart, I am strong, I am tender, I am open hearted. I am perfectly imperfect in this body, right here and right now. I am *not* a picture in a magazine; I am *not* an actress on a movie screen. I stand before you vulnerable and open. I love my body and all that is does for me, for you, for us and for our children." Do you have the courage to claim your truth? Do you have the courage to do it standing naked and vulnerable?

When you claim your Goddess to your partner there is no guarantee that he is ready to hear it. And he may jump up and down with joy, knowing that is the truth and he has been waiting for you to catch on! You will never know unless you claim it. I did not know how to claim my Goddess because at the time I believed that I was not worthy. That partnership ended in a divorce. I knew to say "no more," but I didn't know what came after that.

I spent a lot of years thinking it was him that was "wrong." What I found on my journey was it was also me. I allowed it to happen and he may not have known any better. I must stand up for myself and claim my own Goddess. When I walk in that space, people will either see it or they won't. My only responsibility is to be the most that I can be, know my own Divinity and to love from that place. When I own the Goddess that I am, I attract the man that honors me as the Goddess-because he is able to see his own Divinity. We recognize it in each other and we create a beautiful Divine partnership.

It is time to change what we think it is to be a Goddess. What it means to be a phenomenal woman. It is born from the inside and *explodes* out; not the other way around.

Getting your Goddess Groove on is about owning and being responsible for your life and how you see yourself. Your Goddess Groove is about claiming your own Divinity – your phenomenalness!

I love the Maya Angelou poem "Phenomenal Woman." Here is the first part of the poem:

Pretty women wonder where my secret lies.
I'm not cute or built to suit a fashion model's size
But when I start to tell them,
They think I'm telling lies.
I say,
It's in the reach of my arms
The span of my hips,
The stride of my step,
The curl of my lips.
I'm a woman
Phenomenally.
Phenomenal woman,
That's me.

Are you ready to be a phenomenal woman? Doesn't this sound like a Goddess? Maya Angelou has her Goddess Groove on for sure!

If we want the world to change, not only about what is perceived as beautiful, but in any way, we have to know that it all starts deep within us. I know this may sound simple, and I think the most profound things are simple. I believe that all issues can be solved simply by solving them within ourselves. If we want peace in the world, we must start with peace within ourselves. Then we create peace within our family. Then we create peace within our community of close friends. Then we create peace within our larger community. When we do this, we create a higher vibration within ourselves, and that changes the vibration wherever we go. As we shift our energy into a place of peace, peace starts to show up wherever we go.

This is the same with beauty, love, abundance. It's all the same. Own what it is you want and you will see a shift happen, not only in yourself, but in those around you. And as you see it happen in yourself and in others, you will notice that it ripples out into the world!

You will also begin to notice the law of attraction working. Not only will you start to see a shift in others, you will begin to attract other Goddesses into your life. Have you noticed when you talk endlessly about dieting, or what's wrong with your body, you have an abundance of people to complain with? As you shift into talking about and thinking about the Goddess that you are, you will attract other people into your life that will talk and think the same way.

Who knows where they will show up, but show up they will! Getting your Goddess Groove on opens the door to creating new relationships with others who have their Goddess Groove on! Yummy!

"It's also very helpful to realize that this body that we have, that's sitting right here, right now...with its aches and its pleasures... is exactly what we need to be fully human, fully awake, fully alive."

—Pema Chodron

Oneness-Or, Let's Get Naked!

In my spiritual practice I believe that we are One with each other, with nature, with Source. If I am that, how can I feel anything but good and loving about myself? How can I love nature and all of the unusual and unique facets of nature and not like my own body? When I do this, I am creating separation instead of Oneness.

In trying to come to terms with how I felt about myself and my body, I did a lot of soul searching and nothing was working for me. In my head, I knew it to be true, but I did not *embody* the self love of my physical body. Until . . .

I saw this on a Facebook post from a friend, James Scolari (James Scolari Photography):

"Welcome to the discussion forum for my Skin Deep Photo Sessions, an ongoing nude photography project that endeavors to explore the inner beauty of Venturans from all walks of life, all shapes and sizes. My goal is to photograph nudes for the next ninety days or so, and then mount a show in a local gallery sometime in late summer to benefit worthy local charity.

Models are free to explore anything they like in the shoots; the only requirement is that they be completely nude. No model will participate in the show without consent, nor will any given photo be included without the same consent. Some may find they wish to model but NOT be in the show at all; that's fine, too

Please join the conversation, and please consider my invitation to join me in the studio or on location; all you have to do is leave your clothes at the door. :)."

When I saw this post it was most intriguing. I knew that I could never, ever, do it and I was curious who would do it.

Yes, I was curious, and the more I thought about it and participated and read the discussions about it, the more I started to think about how healing this could be. I saw so much pain about how people perceive their bodies. Pain about not wanting to do things simply because they didn't think they looked good enough. Pain about not wanting to be in a relationship because they would have to get naked to make love. Pain about if someone actually saw the cellulite and then wouldn't want anything to do with them. Pain about people laughing if their naked picture was seen. Pain about wanting to go to the beach, but not going because they would have to put on a swim suit.

I realized that I had some of the same issues. I knew that I did not love my body and was embarrassed by it. Yes, somehow this photo shoot could be healing.

The seed was planted that maybe I could do this. Could I find the inner beauty in myself and also see the beauty of my body just as it is right now? Could I do this without going on a crash diet to lose 20 pounds (or more) so that I could look better in the photographs? Could I see my body as a magnificent body that gets me through every day, just as I am? Could I actually see and honor my body as being a Divine Instrument that carries the essence of who I am?

You know what happens when seeds are planted? They start to grow.

This idea started to grow and started to bring up all sorts of things in me. Of course, the "not good enough, what will people think, only beautiful people will do this and I will be laughed out of town" bullshit came up for me. I began to feel that what was really true was that those thoughts were lies.

I wanted to do this! And I decided I wanted to do it in nature. Nature is the mirror that reflects back to us in such beautiful ways. Everything we see in nature is beautiful. Have you ever wanted to change the way a tree looks? Have you ever thought that a tree is too fat and should lose some of its mass? (I am not talking about a tree in your yard that you are landscaping.) I am talking about what you see naturally in nature.

How about a fish? You know those puffer fish? Do you say, wow we need to change that fish, it sure is ugly and needs to be changed? Or how about an ape? Too hairy, don't you think? Maybe we should shave him—not to mention how big he is!

No. We look at them and we admire the workmanship of these creations. Why do we not do this for ourselves??? Why do we want to change everything? Breast size, too little/too big. Nose, too little too/big. Weight, too much/not enough. Or what about those wonderful lines that tell the world we have lived and laughed?

I decided to pose. This started to bring up a lot in me. The night before the shoot, my husband and I got into a huge fight. As usual, the fight wasn't about what we were fighting about. When we finally got to the truth about what was going on for me, it came to this simple thing. "If I was to pose naked, and he or anyone else saw these pictures, they would know that I am not perfect, that I am not good enough and therefore they would not love me. And if he saw those pictures, he would run so far and so fast because he would truly see me for who I am."

The funny part of this is the fact that he sees me naked every day. But somehow, if it were on paper he would *really* see. And then it would be over.

When I felt this and told him out loud, when I became *vulnerable* and spoke my truth no matter how crazy, that's when I felt a melting and a breakthrough within myself. I was ready to go out there and do this.

This is really important-*vulnerability* is the juice of life. When we can show up and be vulnerable and show what is going on inside, no matter how crazy or weird, we become intimate and there is no amount of "perfect" that can ever achieve that. And I found that revealing my innermost fears and thoughts to him was very healing. He held me and laughed that sweet laugh (not making fun of laugh), the laugh of delight in me and told me he loved me as he wrapped his arms around me.

I asked him to join me on the shoot. I trust him. I also totally trust the photographer. I believe he is wanting to do good and to change the way we think about our bodies. Trust is big and this would not work if I did not trust myself or the photographer.

We went to a great location, a river up in the mountains. It was one of those beautiful blue sky days. The greens were that fresh spring green, the sky was that deep blue sky with white fluffy clouds and the water was clear and beautifully flowing.

I walked down to the water, shedding my clothes. As I dipped my toes into the water, I saw teeny little fish. When I looked up from the water, taking in the beauty that was all around me something happened in my body. I became One with what I was seeing. I was One with the grasses, One with the water, One with the tiny fish swimming in the river, One with the birds flying overhead, One with the trees, One with the rocks. This was not a "head" thing. This was a direct experience, an embodiment of knowing the Truth. We ARE One with the Universe, Spirit, Infinite Being, God.

In this knowing, I waded into the water with my husband as the photographer snapped away. I was in the joy of the moment and loving being there and being naked. I wanted to pose! I wanted to experience all that was around me! I was BEAUTIFUL and I loved myself and everything around me. I felt like I was more alive than I have ever been. I did not waste one minute, not one second, worrying about cellulite, rolls or sagging breasts. I have never felt so free and so totally in the moment, splashing and playing in the water with my husband.

There was a moment when he was looking at me with such love and affection and that puzzled me. I asked why he was looking at me like that. He said, "I always look at you like that." In that moment I knew that because I was loving myself, *I was open to receiving love from him.*

The next day we went to the photographers to look at the pictures. This was huge for me. We were going to look at the pictures on a big screen and we were going to choose the ones we really liked. I was nervous because I am a deleter. In the past, I have deleted most of my pictures because I didn't like how I looked in the picture. Maybe my arms looks a little flabby, my neck a little wrinkly, my stomach too fat. I deleted not only the picture, but also the memory of the event that was taking place. That is so sad for me because I was not only deleting the moment, I was deleting me. Are you a deleter?

So I thought that even though I had such an amazing day, I would end up deleting the pictures. All of them.

When we arrived at the photographers, we sat down and started to look at the pictures. I did not delete one picture. It was the first time that I ever saw myself as beautiful. Not because of make-up or clothes or because the lighting was just right. It was because I was glowing from within and I knew that I was beautiful. I saw myself as the Divine Being that I am.

This is not the end of the story. There was another part to the Face Book post: "Mount a show." Yes, there was a show. At first I thought that meant that he would mount a few of the pictures and hang them somewhere. I was thinking it would be like the local art shows that I have gone to before. A few pictures, small pictures, mounted on a local gallery wall where no one would be very interested in going.

This was not the case. If you can, imagine a twenty by twenty foot screen. Yes, twenty feet high and twenty feet across. Now imagine images projected on this screen. This very big screen. This was his idea of mounting a show.

The show was local and it was advertised-which meant people would come. There was a private showing for all of the models and I was pretty nervous about it. It was absolutely fantastic! We were all in this together, we had all stepped waaaayyy out of our comfort zone and we all looked fabulous. I believe James fulfilled his wish to show that beauty was so much more than skin deep!

After the private showing, it was opened to the public. Standing there, talking to friends and people I didn't know, with my picture up on the screen, was an experience I will never forget. People saw and acknowledged the beauty in each and every one of us. It was weird, but more than that it was freeing. It was a declaration of standing naked, vulnerable and open. *Here I am.* I am willing to show you me. Are you willing to show me you? (Not naked, but vulnerable?)

In doing this show one of the things that I experienced as Truth is that we are all Divine and we are all unique in these bodies. We are all Beautiful.

There is a great quote from Ernest Holmes: *"for all you have to do is to look about in nature and find that while everything comes from one source, everything bears the stamp of a unique individuality. The great lesson that life is trying to teach us is that we are all rooted in God, but each is an individualized center in the Divine Being. We have what Emerson calls unity at the center and variety at the circumference. Unity does not mean uniformity. Unity means a oneness of purpose."*

The beauty in nature is simply a reflection of YOU!

That is what I was feeling on the photo shoot. My individuality and beauty. I was a part of nature. As each thing in nature was beautiful, so was I. As each thing in nature was unique, so was I.

I am from Source, as is everything in nature and I am not like the trees or the fish. I am like me. Each tree is different, each fish is different, and each person is different. Some fish are large and colorful and some are small and white. Some trees flower and some trees are gnarled and lose their leaves. Some people have dark skin and some people have light skin.

What if the beauty in nature is simply a reflection of you?

I am not the same as you physically, nor you the same as me. How boring it would be if we were all the same. When we look at the diversity in nature, we honor it and we love it. When we look at the diversity in the human body, we make fun of and disrespect that which is different. More often than not, we do that to ourselves. I want this to stop for me. I want to claim that I am me and I am perfect as I am.

I can hear you now. "But what if I really am fat? Or what if I have acne? Or what if I am too thin? Or all of the other things that a body is? What if I'm too hairy? How can you say I'm perfect?" I can say it because you are not your body. You are not your fat, your hair, your acne, your too thinness. You are the Divine Presence. Your body is your body, here to be used to experience the Infinite Being that you are. You are here to experience the infinite possibilities of this reality, this earthly plane. You have nothing to change or to fix because you are not broken. How can an Infinite Divine Being ever be broken? Seriously. How?

What if, before you look into the mirror, you asked to be shown something beautiful today? And then you looked into the mirror and what you were shown was you, the beautiful being that you are. What if?

Does that mean I don't have to work out and eat healthy foods? NO. It doesn't mean that at all.

When you get to the point where you honor yourself for where you are in your body and you see the Divine presence in yourself, you will want to treat your body like the temple that it is.

Think about the vessel that your body is. It carries the unique and Divine energy, the God-ness of you. When you see that and really feel that, you will do what you need to do to take care of this human body!

In this new age of spiritual awakening, we as humans, have begun to think that we are here to become spiritual beings. The truth is that we are Divine Infinite Beings. We *are* that. We do not need to *become* that. What we are here to do, as Infinite Beings, is to be human. To be in this human body and everything that means. We are here to experience life to its fullest and to embody experiences and sensations!

Stop for a minute and feel what it feels like to have these experiences:

- ➢ ocean breezes on your face
- ➢ sun shining on your body
- ➢ the taste of yummy foods
- ➢ the glory of movement
- ➢ the enchanting sound of music
- ➢ the joy of dance
- ➢ the orgasm of sex
- ➢ the gentleness of touch
- ➢ the warm embrace of a child
- ➢ the feeling of a baby sleeping on your chest
- ➢ the pain of a loss
- ➢ the thrill of a roller coaster
- ➢ the butterflies of stepping into the unknown
- ➢ the anticipation of a close match in a sports game
- ➢ the pride of accomplishment

We need a body to experience all of these luscious things. By being fully present and in our bodies-loving our bodies, we get to experience all of these things because we are living life in a big way. Isn't that why we are here-to embody our bodies?

We each chose to come into these bodies so that we could experience the sensations and goodness that these bodies allow-things that our Spiritual beings cannot. How cool is that? We chose to be here and embody life and lusciousness!

Getting your Goddess Groove on means not wasting any of the juiciness of life on not being enough! So get over it already and get *your Goddess Groove on!* How yummy is that?

"The purpose of my life is to shimmer and to radiate love to those around me through my dance of life."

—Maria Bucaro

Healing The Wounds

One of the very first things we do in the preparation phase of a vision quest is to look at our wounds. It is not important to dig up old wounds to grow and expand. It is not important to figure out each and every detail of what our pain is and what caused it. It *is* important to be conscious of past wounds, knowing that they exist and in that consciousness we can shift from pain to peace. We can shift from being pissed off, or pieced off, separate and in pain, into wholeness.

When stuff does come up, it is good to see it, deal with it and continue on the path. Healing some wounds can heal many wounds, so when an opportunity comes up for healing, jump on it. Diving in can reveal many gifts!

The story that I told you about being in Orchesis in high school is an example of what I am talking about. That was a very deep wound. I gave someone so much power over me and it showed up in a lot of ways throughout my life. Healing that wound has helped to heal other wounds.

Sometimes we never know what it is that will heal. Forgiveness is often a very good start to healing. Forgiving the person who we feel wronged us, as well as forgiving ourselves. I was able to start the healing of that "dance wound" by forgiving him for his attitude and how he treated me. I did this many times over, thinking it was all about forgiving him.

A few years ago, in a class I was taking, we did a large piece on forgiveness. This dancing issue came up again and I questioned how many times I would need to forgive him. It finally hit me that it was not him I needed to forgive-it was me. I needed to forgive myself for allowing him treat me that way. I needed to forgive myself for giving up dancing. I needed to forgive myself for losing my voice and living my life with no self-expression. And so I did. I forgave myself. And there was more.

I decided to open myself up, to be vulnerable and to dance. Since that day, back in high school, I never danced in public and it was very rare that I danced at all. In this class, the final project was whatever we wanted it to be-it just needed to express something we had gotten out of the class. I decided to dance my final project. To say that I was nervous and scared would hardly describe my fear. And yet I knew it was something that I had to do. I found music that I loved and choreographed a dance. I told the class the story of why I was doing this and then I danced my heart out. I danced like there was no one watching and like everyone was watching. I soared and I healed. I finished to a standing ovation and my heart sang. This was magic and this was joy.

And it gets even better. My husband knew what I was doing and why. He could not be there to witness my dance, my coming out. But he did give me a beautiful card that expressed his seeing and acknowledging what I did. He said *"I thought of you dancing your heart out and I know it was beautiful and I wish I could have seen it. I am very proud of you and know I am deeply blessed that you are my wife."* Being seen and witnessed not only by my classmates, but also by my husband was very healing. We all want to be seen and to be loved for who we are.

And it gets even better. A few years later I was dancing with Kate Nash in a Nia class at Cosmotion. The theme of the dance was dancing "what if." During the dance, as Kate was cuing us to dance "what if," it suddenly came to me. What if, when I was sixteen, my boyfriend told me that my dance was beautiful and he was proud of me? What if? What if he didn't say that it was great and I responded with my own knowing that my dance was beautiful, and I didn't need to hear him say it? What if I stood in my truth? What if I chose to live my life, fully expressing? In that moment, in the class, I danced in full self-expression and in that moment, I healed even more. Time was erased and I felt whole and complete.

(Please note the distinction in the "what if." I am not talking about "if only I would have done___" or "what if I would have said ____" or "what if this had never happened." It is not about beating yourself up. I am talking about expanding out into the possibilities of "what if." It is expansive, rather than contractive.)

I did not go out seeking to heal this wound. When it was presented to me, I opened up to the possibility of seeing things in a different way-a different point of view. I took action that empowered me and I forgave. This was another way to slay the beast of "not enough!" (You'll learn about slaying the beast a little later in the book.)

When you feel heavy with an old story or an old way of being, consider opening up to the possibility of changing the story. Is there something you could do to heal the old wound?

By the way, what do you think this story has to do with loving your body?

Powerful Purpose And Ways Of Being

How do you want to be in the world? Who do you want to be when you wake up in the morning? What drives you? What does that even mean?

Do you want to do what makes you happy? Do you want to *be* what makes you happy? When we know who we are and what we want, we live our lives in joy and no one can take that away from us. Not even if someone makes a nasty comment or judgment about our body!

Having a purpose, a priority in life helps to relieve stress and creates an ease in life because we know what is important to us and all decisions are made from that place.

When I did that mastery event that I spoke of earlier, I had no idea what my purpose in life was. During the event, there was an exercise that we did which was to come up with the purpose of our lives. I knew it wasn't to be a "something." By that I mean my purpose wasn't to be a realtor or a writer or a speaker. I knew it was much deeper than being an occupation.

My purpose was so far from who and what I was and yet I knew it was right for me. I left there knowing that I would someday walk into it.

That was in January 2001. Ever since then, I have been creating circumstances and events that have been opening me to living my purpose. I am now walking and living my purpose that was created with no idea of what it even meant when I created the words-and along with the words were the feelings that were associated with it.

My purpose, as written in January, 2001 was:

The purpose of my life is to shimmer and to radiate love to those around me through my dance of life.

I really did not know what this meant. I didn't know how to do it. It may sound simple, and to me it was profound. As part of the exercise I needed to say it until the rest of my group believed it to be true for me. When I finally got to say it as it is written above, I believed it and so did they.

I did not know how to start to shimmer. I wasn't even sure what it meant to shimmer. I knew I had to take an action in order to begin to walk into this statement. The first thing I could think of doing was to create my email address of "shimmeringnow@." I still use this address for my personal address. It reminds me daily of my purpose.

As I have been expanding in who I am, I realized that I cannot shimmer or radiate anything if I do not love myself. How can I dance through life if I am "yucking" myself? Part of loving me is being me, as I am, right now. There is nothing that I need to do differently (lose weight, have a different nose, erase the wrinkles) to love myself right now. When I love myself just as I am and see the beauty in myself, just as I am, I open up to shimmering and radiating the love that I feel for myself to those around me. It does make me want to dance. My life is a dance. I am living my purpose.

Knowing my purpose helps me to stay on track. If I am thinking my purpose is about guiding, or writing a book, and I'm being not pleasant to be around because I am trying to get something done, then I am not living my purpose. I can stand back, breathe and know that these are only vehicles for me to live my purpose.

If you don't know what your purpose is, take some time and feel into what it is. It will be a feeling first and then the words will come. Why are you here? Here's a clue. It isn't to make money or be better at your job.

Are you someone who doesn't believe you have a purpose? Do you live your life thinking that everyone else has a purpose being here and you don't? Believe it or not, you do. If you want to discover your purpose in life, you must first realize that you do have a purpose, even if you don't know what it is yet. Let go of the belief that you are not worthy of living powerfully and purposefully, just for now.

You can discover your purpose in life just like I did. There are many ways to do this, but what we did at the seminar was pretty simple and you can do this with friends. Be open to this process, and it will work for you. Here's what to do:

1. Stand in a circle of friends.
2. One person at a time says, "My purpose in life is_____." The first person continues saying "my purpose is" until their purpose is truly stated. Then continue on to the next person. Do not move on until the process is completed.
3. Say whatever pops into your head. It doesn't have to be a complete sentence or make any sense.
4. Keep going until you say the purpose that makes you cry and whatever it is you feel when you hear the Truth spoken (hair

standing on the back of your neck or a feeling in your gut)This is your purpose.

5. Say your purpose until your group is moved because they heard the Truth spoken and they believe you. This should go without saying that you have gathered a group whom you trust and that you hold each other in grace and love.

The first answers that you come up with will be your "should" or programmed answers, or the social conditioning answers about what you think your purpose in life is. These are not your purpose. They are just answers that come from the little mind. Your true answer is Divinely Guided and you will know that it comes directly from Source.

When you finally get to your purpose it will resonate with you deeply, as well as with those supporting you. Your purpose will have a special energy to you, and you will feel that energy whenever you speak it.

His Holiness the Dalai Lama says that the reason we are here is to express joy and to be happy. What rings true for you?

Once you know your purpose, you will begin to live your life ever moving into that purpose. You will begin to live your life with new ways of being.

Remember that this is all about creating portals for you to walk through so that you will have a direct experience of *Truth*.

The following exercises and ways of being may be openings to new ways of being in your body. Go through them and see what feels light to do. As you play with and experiment with who you are and who you are walking into, do if from the place of standing in the power of purpose.

Have fun-and please don't take yourself or any of this too seriously. I think it's important for all of us, myself included, to lighten up and just be. Getting your Goddess Groove on is fun, sexy, light hearted and yummy!

"As a society, we need to get lots more flexible about what constitutes beauty. It isn't a particular hair color or a particular body type; it's the woman who grew the hair and lives in the body. Keeping this in mind can only make things better. "

—Victoria Moran

Why Don't I Like How I Look? Where Does it Come From?

Are these even good questions to ask? Maybe that is part of the problem! How about a question like: How can I love my body even more today? Does that sound a little more empowering? How about: When I delight in my body, what does that feel like? Getting your Goddess Groove on is about asking empowering questions that delight.

The truth is, we are the only ones that can make ourselves *not* feel good about anything. How do we get there when there are so many outside influences?

We are inundated with marketing and advertising that tells us what looks good and what is beautiful. Our culture tells us what is acceptable and beautiful.

Our body image also comes from a long time ago. Our thoughts and ways of being may not even be our own thoughts and feelings. Maybe they came from mom, a sister, a friend, or from life times ago. Think about when you were young and how easily you may have been influenced.

As children we were very susceptible to words, looks or actions that were directed toward us. Even if those words or actions were not directed toward us, the energy that was created from others, opened up the space for us to feel negatively about ourselves and our bodies.

How did your parents feel about their bodies? How did your friends feel about their bodies? How does your family feel about each other? Are you judged on your appearance?

In my family, when we get together, the first thing everyone does is look you over. You know what I mean. It's the look from head to toe, assessing if weight was gained, hair was lost and general overall appearance. My guess is that most families do this. It is not done to be mean or critical, it is a way of being. It is a learned behavior. Because it is so implanted in me, I still find myself starting to do it when I see people, not just family members. I must take a moment, breathe, and then remember that I am not about that.

When I see that I am being assessed, I used to immediately go into the thoughts of "I am not good enough." This type of behavior preys on the "not good enough" that so many of us feel. Now, I can smile and know that it does not matter one little bit what someone else thinks. I have no need to measure up to someone else's idea of how I look or should look.

Love your body now, and you will release any hold anyone else has on how *you* feel about *your* body!

Steps To Changing Body Image

So lets get down to it. If you don't feel good about your body what can you do to change the image that you see?

Remember that transformation does not happen in your head. It does not happen because you study a course in _____(fill in the blank) or because someone else tells you "how" to transform old ways of being. Transformation happens when you open up to the possibility of transformation and the possibility of a direct experience. When you question what else is possible, new ways of being present themselves and this is what you can step into. You can step into the true joy that you are; the beauty and the Goddess that you are *right now*!!!

But what if you aren't embodying loving your body right now? Here are some things that may open up a portal for you to walk through and have a direct experience of the truth-the truth that you are already perfect. If that little voice is still going and telling you that you can't possibly love your body now, try some of these exercises in the next chapters.

Questions are always a great way to start. Here are some steps that may be helpful:

> ➢ Discover your strengths and weaknesses—What do you love about your body? What do you hate about your body? Take some time to journal these now. Then do the mirror exercises that are explained later in the book.

> ➢ What beliefs do you have about what is beautiful and where do those beliefs come from? Do the belief exercises that are explained later in the book.

> ➢ What about now? What is beauty? Do the belief exercises.

> ➢ Speak what you think. Say out loud what you think about your body (as in the mirror exercises, Loo Zer exercise, Voices of the Past exercise found later in the book).

> ➢ Feel what you think. Really get into the feelings. This is not about your head and thinking it through! Do you feel shame? Guilt? Pain? Hate?

> ➢ Slay the beast, which is a way of *demanding that change is necessary right now!* – more about that later.

> ➢ Heal what you think.

> ➢ Change what you think and change the voice. Speak your truth now.

> ➢ Change your voice and change the world.

"Do something every day that is loving toward your body and gives you the opportunity to enjoy the sensations of your body."

—Golda Poretsky

Rites Of Passage And Grief

One night as I was lying in bed, I had my arm down around my stomach as I have many times before. I remembered when I used to be able to put my arm in the same place and it wouldn't touch my stomach because there was no poochiness there at all. It used to be a measure, more than a scale, of how I was doing. If I could place my arm in a certain place and just feel air, I was okay. I was not conscious of what "I was okay" meant. Now I know that it meant I was worthy.

Feeling the tum, I started to cry, which led to the sob of grief. I was grieving the young woman I used to be. I was even grieving the 50 year old woman I used to be. When it was over, I realized that we don't acknowledge, let alone grieve many of the losses that we have as we move through life. I was in the middle of a rite of passage.

A rite of passage is a ritual event that marks a person's transition from one status to another. By that I mean any kind of life changing event, from small events to really big ones. Things like puberty, birthdays, graduations, marriage, divorce, children leaving the house, a new job and even the body taking on different proportions are all considered to be rites of passage. It is a death and a re-birth.

The thing that is missing in our culture is the ritual part. Often times we don't even acknowledge the rite of passage, let alone create a ritual around it and honor what was and what is.

A vision quest is considered to be a rite of passage in itself. And a vision quest is an event that is used to mark rites of passage. Since I have become a vision quest Guide, I now look at all of life as a quest. Almost everything we do is a death and a re-birth.

What does this have to do with loving your body? A lot.

The death for me was having a body that said middle age, which in part looks like gray hair, sagging skin and wrinkles. The process is about moving from how I had always considered myself, having a youthful body, into being at peace and acceptance with where I am with my body now. To be reborn with the love and the passion for myself in terms way bigger than a few wrinkles, gray hair and some tummy rolls. To love my body now, simply because it is my body. And it was about the loss of youth, crazy dieting and even the loss of "not enough." How crazy is that? It seems crazy, but it is actually a loss and a transformation. Even though it is something I choose and I want, it is still something to be acknowledged and grieved. It is a death and re-birth.

Death deserves tears. They can be tears of sorrow or tears of joy. It all depends on what your point of view is about death. We do need to grieve the losses in our lives, which means they need to be acknowledged. We cannot just get over grief. Grief is something that must be lived, acknowledged and moved through. We cannot just clear it and get over it. There is magic in feeling the grief, moving through it and coming out the other side.

I needed to take time to know and to feel the feelings of knowing that I will never be 20 years old again, or 30 or 40 or 50. More than likely I will never have that super flat stomach and weigh 120 pounds. I could if I wanted to. But in this moment, I choose to not do what it would take to do that. Can that change tomorrow? Absolutely.

I am moving into being 60. What is the re-birth? What is possible as I enter into my 6th decade? Yes, this is a rite of passage!

On the other end of life and transition, when a girl goes through puberty and has her first lady days, (thank you Shawna and Genny for that term!) she is dying to the young girl and her body is preparing for womanhood. Well, okay that is true, but back in the day when girls were getting married in their mid teens and having kids then it was more about preparing for womanhood. Now, it is still a really big event in a girl's life and it is considered to be a rite of passage, but womanhood is still a long way off. As a culture we do not celebrate a young girl getting her period, and there is no ritual that usually takes place.

This happened for me when I was ten. I can remember standing on my front porch and my Dad came out to talk to me. I was so happy that he wanted to talk to me and I thought that this was something special. What he said was, "You are not my little girl anymore, you are now a young woman and you need to behave like one" and the feeling that I attached was "My life is over and my Dad doesn't love me anymore." I can't say that at this time in my life I am clear what he meant when he said it, and I am sure he did not mean what I attached to it. What I felt was the "death" part but it was not balanced with the re-birth part in a way that I could understand. There was no celebration.

I think that if my first period was marked as a rite of passage, I would have been a lot more comfortable with the changes my body was going through when I was ten. I may not have needed to hide in a sweater in the heat. Even the school could have been notified to put a container in the bathrooms to dispose of kotex pads (yes, this was before tampons), which were not in the elementary schools.

Rites of Passage

A rite of passage has three components: Severance, Threshold and Incorporation/Integration. Anything that you go through in life has these components if you look for them.

A reminder:

Severance is the time of letting go of what no longer works for you. What are you holding on to that is keeping you back? This is the time to separate from old ways of being. What are you letting go of?

Threshold is the in between time. Think of the threshold at the door. You are neither in nor out. This is the time to learn and to play with what is coming up. In a vision quest, this is the time on the mountain where everything is left behind and you get to dance in the spirit world. This is the time of fasting and letting go of everything that feels comfortable. This is where you die to the old and embrace the new. Death and re-birth.

Incorporation is the time of living the new way of being. It is often said that incorporation is the most difficult of the three phases because this is where you walk your talk. Who are you now?

How can you apply the rites of passage to loving your body?

One of my favorite things to do is a day walk. If you can set aside a whole day, that's great! If you only have time for a half of a day, that will work, too. The idea is to give yourself the gift of time and the gift of going deep within.

A day walk is a day of journeying into nature and into your own being. (A hike into the mountains, beach, park-whatever you have access to.) It is time to still the mind and look upon nature to reflect back to you the inner journey that you are going on. This is the place of the threshold-the in-between time-and can be a very mystical and magical experience.

The first thing to do is to find a place in nature that is not highly populated. When you go on your day walk, it is all about going inward. You do not want to be talking to people and have a lot going on around you. As much as you might want to, don't bring your dog. You do not want to focus on anything else but you. If you bring a friend to do this with, separate at the threshold. This time is all about you!

Before going out, take some time to decide what you are dying to. What are you marking in your life regarding your body? What is it that you want to let go?

Ideally, you will want to arrive at your place in nature just as the sun is rising, arriving back to your car just before sunset. This would be a perfect time to fast which means you don't have to carry any food! Do carry an emergency kit, which should include some simple things like Band-Aids, a lighter, mole skin and a rain poncho. Be sure to bring plenty of water, at least 3 quarts to one gallon so that you can drink throughout the day. A journal is a good idea so that you can write the story of your walk. I love to bring a hammock, too. Keep your load light enough to just carry a day pack-not a full-on back pack. Also be sure to tell someone where you are going and when you expect to return.

As you go into nature, literally mark a threshold. This can be drawing a line in the dirt, stepping over a stick, walking between two rocks—you get the idea. What you are doing is leaving (severance) the world behind and entering a time of the mystical and magical world.

There should be no destination or goal in mind. You can hike, meander, nap, bring a hammock and swing, sit on a rock or whatever your intuition tells you to do. How awesome to take the time to wander intuitively. Observe what you see in the rocks, trees, insects, birds. Are there stories to be told? Be still and be curious and listen. Observe what you see in your body. How is your body working for you? How does your body feel, lying in the grass looking up at the clouds? Are you in a place private enough to be naked? What does that feel like? Can you dance with the trees? Can you sing with the river?

Go inside and look to see if there is anything that needs to be grieved. Do you need to cry, to sob, to howl? What is in you that wants to be released?

Explore what it means to die to an old way of being. Feel what is being born in you. Is there a ritual you might like to do that will mark the transition from an old way of being (death) into a new way of being (birth)?

When you return to the threshold, again consciously cross with gratitude to yourself and to Mother Earth for holding you, and any lessons that were taught along the way.

When you get back, you can share your story with a loved one. This is so great because you get to be seen and they can mirror back to you any parts of the story that you may not have seen as significant!

If this appeals to you, you may be ready for a vision quest. A vision quest consists of a preparation phase where you are prepared to go to the mountain; learning how to physically be on the mountain, how to fast for four days and four nights - (it's so not about the food!) and learn about safety and your gear. In other words, the logistics. This is happening during your severance phase where you are also preparing for the death that is coming.

The next phase is being on the mountain. You will find your spot where you will fast alone in the wilderness, calling upon your ancestors and communing with Source. This is your threshold phase. Here you will seek your vision and find your gift that you will bring back to the world.

The next phase is incorporation. This is when you come back to your world, your people. This is where you live your vision and give your gift.

Do you hear the mountain calling? Yes? Please contact me for more information!

Thoughts Create

In his book *Messages in Water*, Dr. Masaru Emoto wrote of his discoveries on water crystals. He discovered that the crystals formed in frozen water revealed changes when specific, concentrated thoughts are directed toward them. He found that water that had been exposed to loving words shows brilliant, complex snowflake patterns. Water exposed to negative thoughts, forms incomplete, asymmetrical patterns with dull colors.

So I'm thinking that since our bodies are 70% water, why not create beautiful water crystals in our bodies?

This is not scientific-what I am saying is we can create anything we want-why not create the image of our bodies as beautiful water crystals?

In case you are not sure or can't come up with what you would like to be, here is a list to stir your imagination. Start from this list and get fun and creative with your own list! Remind yourself daily:

I AM:

Beautiful	Peace
Strong	Love
Courageous	Creative
Confident	Playful
Sexy	Inspiring
Sensuous	Compassionate
Radiant Light	Blessed
Joy	Magnetic
Lighthearted	Soulful
Passionate	Juicy

I Am

I Am is a full and complete sentence. You have probably heard the statement "I Am, that I Am."

That is true and no more definition is needed. You are, I am, Divine Source, Infinite Being and more than our bodies We are not our bodies and we have bodies. So, who are you in your body?

Who are You in your everyday living? You get to define who you are and you get to do it without the influence of anyone else. Not your culture, or society or even your partner in life.

You can create your life in any way that you want. And if you don't create your life consciously, you are still creating it anyway.

Create who you want to be.

Do you want to be beautiful? Do you want to be strong? Do you want to be sensuous? Do you want to be sexy? Do you want to be confident? Do you want to be radiant light? Do you want to love yourself? Do you want to be love? Do you want to be joyful? Do you want to be funny? Do you want to be inspiring? Do you want to be playful? Do you want to be magnetic?

Get your Goddess Groove on and decide who you want to be. Make it yummy!

Who are you?

I am_____

I am_____

I am_____

I am_____

I am_____

I am_____

I am_____

I am_____

I am_____

I am_____

I am_____

Slaying The Beast

Slaying the beast is all about finding the Spiritual Warrior within and getting rid of whatever keeps you from being the Goddess that you truly are.

Slaying the beast is making a demand that something needs to change and it needs to change "now." When we want something to change, we must be clear and we must be willing to do whatever it takes.

Notice the feeling that is evoked with "I'd kind of like to feel different and be different. It would be nice to love my body at some point." Now feel the power of the word demand. "I choose to love my body now, and I demand that my self-loathing changes – right here and right now!" Demanding is a way to open up a portal for a direct experience. And of course, that is where change and transformation happen.

When we make a demand, we don't need to know how or what to do. The process of making a demand opens the door to possibilities. Spirit/Universe takes over and delivers life events that create a direct experience simply because a demand is full of emotion. Emotion and feelings are an open door for transformation.

I discovered "slaying the beast" when I was on my own vision quest. Clif and I, along with a group of other vision quest guides went into the desert to do what is called a "renewal fast." It is a gift that is given by other guides who come and guide us, after our time of guiding others. It is a gift that is greatly appreciated!

On this fast, it was our intention to fast as a couple in order to learn how to guide other couples through the vision quest process. This was interesting and is a topic of another conversation. We did learn, and came up with some great ideas for couple's fasting, but I got so much more out of this fast.

On the second day of the fast I was sitting peacefully, looking out over the mountains. I found a beautiful spot to just sit and be. I was at peace soaking in the beauty. This spot was special to me because I am a mountain person, not so much a desert person. In this spot was a pine tree, and that lone tree felt like home amidst the yucca, scrub and Joshua trees.

As I gazed out at the mountains, sitting quietly in the silence of the high desert, I learned that the desert has much to offer. Out of nowhere I started to weep. At first I couldn't place where the tears were coming from. And then it hit me. I was back in the story of "not enough." I was not deserving to be here with these amazing people, in this amazing place. I could not believe this was coming up again. After all of the work I have done, I thought this issue had been put to bed. I wanted it gone, over and done with! I demanded that this deep feeling of "not enough" be gone from my being.

And then I got mad. I saw this as a "beast of not enough-ness." The only way to get rid of a beast is to slay it.

As women, especially spiritual women, we don't usually like to get into the messiness of beast slaying. It is often felt that it is better to meditate, pray or affirm that we are enough. Trust me, I have done it all. I knew that it was time to find my spiritual warrior and go to war with this beast.

On the third day of my fast, I realized that in order to go to war I needed a weapon. I looked around for a weapon and I found a great branch from cactus. I used a knife to form it and shape it into a powerful sword. The day was spent forming my weapon and my attack strategy.

On the fourth day, I woke up at dawn. I knew that I wanted to be up high and to be facing the East. East on the medicine wheel is the place of death and re-birth. I climbed up the mountain and when I reached the top, the sun was just coming up over the ridge. I faced the East and took off my clothes.

Standing naked on the cold rocks, I greeted the sun. I picked up my sword and asked the spirits of the South, my warrior sisters, to guide me into battle. I called up all of the self-loathing that was within my being. I called up all of the memories of not being good enough.

As I stood there, holding my sword, voices of the past started to come. Images from the past started to come. As each voice or image came, I slayed it. As each thought, word or deed of "not good enough" came to me, I slayed it. And then people came and I slayed them. Never again would I be looked at or talked to with disdain, or smirked at by anyone, not even me, and take it on as true. I cried, I screamed and I struck out, wielding that sword for all I was worth. I kept at it until I was exhausted and there was nothing and no one left to slay.

I slayed the beast. I slayed the beast of negative self-talk. I slayed the beast of beliefs that do not serve me. I slayed the beast of other people keeping me small. They no longer have power over me. I slayed the beast of "not enough." I slayed the beast.

When there was no more, I fell to the ground, an empty vessel. I turned to the North, weeping and I called in the wisdom of the North. I called to God and I sang: *"Here I am. A vessel to be filled. Whatever Spirit needs of me, I will be, I will be I will be."*

I was emptied and filled up again. I spent the rest of the day in rest and integrating what had happened. In fact, I am still integrating and incorporating this profound experience.

This is the beauty of a vision quest. The gift is the time away from phones, computers and people so that I can go deeply into who I am and what is going on in this human body. The gift is to find my own reflection in nature and know the beauty that resides in nature is the beauty that resides in me.

I am worth the time. I am enough. You are worth the time. You are enough. We are worth the time. We are enough.

"Women's magazines ignore older women or pretend that they don't exist; magazines try to avoid photographs of older women, and 'retouching artists' conspire to 'help' beautiful women look more beautiful, less than their age...By now readers have no idea what a real woman's 60 year old face looks like in print because it's made to look 45. Worse, 60 year old readers look in the mirror and think they are too old, because they're comparing themselves to some retouched face smiling back at them from a magazine."

—Dalma Heyn

Voices Of The Past

We carry a lot of negative self-talk and thoughts as a result of voices from the past. A voice from the past is exactly what it sounds like. A voice from the past can be anything that anyone ever said and then you took it as your own thought or belief. This is something to be aware of— we do not need to own and keep other people's thoughts as our own! What a concept. Once we are aware that some thoughts and voices that we hear are not ours, we can get rid of them and send them back.

A voice from the past may not even be about you. It might be something you heard someone say about a friend or sibling and you took it on for yourself. You may have heard something on TV that stuck with you.

For me, one voice from the past was the story about being a model and being in the car with my friends. The voice of my friends mom was the voice that I heard about me not being enough of whatever to be a model.

The voice of the past can be feelings. It can be unspoken rules in your household. As children, we often know without words even being spoken.

In order to move forward we need to find out what voices we are listening to. Are we listening to a voice that we heard when we were five, ten or fifteen years old? This is where our beliefs come from. It is important to know what our beliefs are—we just might need some brain washing!

For many of us, there was a defining moment when we heard something and a belief was formed. Can you remember a time that this is true for you?

Things you will need for this exercise:

> ➢ Paper and pen
> ➢ A good friend to listen and witness

What was the comment/thought/feeling you heard?

_____

_____

_____

_____

Who said it?   Was it someone in your family? A friend? Something on TV or in the media?

_____

_____

How old were you?

_____

How did it feel then?

_____

_____

How does it feel now?

_____

_____

Take some time and write out this story. You can journal it or just write it out as a story. Write it out on paper, don't use the computer.

After you have written your story, be dramatic and set the stage for storytelling. Tell your story to someone that will hold you with love and compassion and witness you. They are not there to fix you or change you, they are only there to listen. This is the last time you will tell this story.

"Telling yourself you like the way you look is easy. Believing it is an entirely different kettle of whales."

—*Andrew Biss*

Loo - Zer

Negative self-talk, that little voice, is often felt and heard coming from over our shoulder and just behind our ears. If you just said "what little voice," that's what I'm talking about. Imagine it is a character that sits on your shoulder, day in and day out. Imagine a face and a voice of this self-talk. This voice has been with you for a long time. I call this voice Loo-Zer. When I first heard about Loo many years ago, I did not believe that Loo was a part of my life. And then I started to notice the endless banter that I always thought was "me" talking.

Loo is the opposite of what I call "God's Whisper" or intuition. Intuition is going beyond the five senses and hearing Divine guidance. God's Whisper is another voice, a voice that you *do* want to listen to. Do not confuse Loo's voice with God's Whisper. Know they are different. When you take a moment to listen and not just act, you will know the difference.

Loo operates from fear. God's Whisper is that voice that comes from within, the knowing of your inner wisdom. Trust your intuition, do not trust Loo!

Here are some of the things Loo thrives on:

- ➢ Not being good enough
- ➢ Being a victim
- ➢ Not taking any risk
- ➢ Hiding out
- ➢ Being resigned
- ➢ Not belonging
- ➢ Feeling doom
- ➢ Feeling bad about everything
- ➢ Being aloof
- ➢ Not bothering
- ➢ Giving up
- ➢ Living in fear
- ➢ Being stingy
- ➢ Living in lack
- ➢ Uncertainty

Loo also wants to remind me that I am certainly not good enough. I am not worthy of anything good. Loo will never stop telling me about all of the times I messed up, got hurt, disappointed someone or failed.

Loo's biggest job of all is to remind me that I am the Biggest Loser out there (and Loo is not referring to the courageous people on the TV show!).

Speaking of weight, Loo will let me know that I don't compare to the models in the magazines, that my body is pathetic and that I don't look good in any type of clothes, let alone look good naked. Loo will make me feel guilty for trying and failing to lose/gain weight–and will tell me right away that I can't do it. And I'm stupid for trying.

Can you see how this applies in your life? Do you hear Loo's voice? Do you listen? Take some time and really think about this.

Loo Zer Exercise

Go inside and listen to some of the things that Loo tells you on a regular basis.

Top Fifteen Things Loo tells me:

1._____
2._____
3._____
4._____
5._____
6._____
7._____
8._____
9._____
10._____
11._____
12._____
13._____
14._____
15._____

After you have created your list of the top 15 things Loo tells you, you will start to see a pattern. Once you are aware of the voice, you can decide if it is something you want to listen to. It is your choice.

For a long time Loo told me that I had no voice. That I had nothing to say, and even if I wanted to talk, no one would want to hear. I remember many times when friends would get together and have amazing discussions on whatever topics-it didn't matter what the topic was-I would not engage in the conversations. Loo told me that what I had to say would be stupid and not as smart as everyone else.

These thoughts were not in alignment of what was really true for me. I knew that I had a lot to say, but I listened to Loo because I did not want to look foolish or say something that would make me look stupid. Not looking stupid was big for me and that goes back to when I was six years old.

My dad was an electrical engineer. As I was growing up he was in school getting his doctorate. In my young mind, fathers didn't come any smarter than him. One night he was helping me with my arithmetic homework. I was six. I needed to add 3 +3, and I could not figure it out. He got so mad at me and let me know that I must be really stupid if I couldn't figure out how much 3 + 3 equaled. I was devastated because this is what he did as an engineer, he worked with numbers, and I was a disappointment because I did not know numbers.

At that moment I decided that I would never open my mouth because I never wanted anyone to know I was stupid. Of course, this was not a conscious decision. Loo was there to take note. Loo's job is to protect me. I was hurt. Loo decided that I should never step out and be stupid and so that I could never be hurt. Much better to be small and safe.

Loo also wanted me to be invisible because being invisible meant no friends, no risk and that equaled safety. This led me to being aloof and arrogant. No one knew me or cared to know me. I was aloof, never said anything and did not let people get to know me, I was assured to not have any friends. No friends = no hurt.

It is important for you to become aware of this voice because Loo will have you think that Loo is not there. Loo wants you to think that *you* are thinking these thoughts. And you are, or at least there is a part of you, the part that wants to keep you safe, which is Loo.

When you become conscious of this voice and know that it is not *who you really are*, you can be free of it. Well, not really free of the voice-it will always be there. But you will be free of thinking you have to listen. You have the freedom of choice of whether you want to listen or not. The first step is to see Loo for what it is.

Everyone has parts that make up the whole of who we are. That little voice, the self-talk, is a part of you and all parts are there to serve a purpose and to take care of you. It's not so much that Loo is wanting "bad" for you or wants you to fail-in fact it's the opposite. Loo is the part that wants to make sure that you are always okay. The problem is that Loo does not know what would be okay for you. Right now Loo may be arguing with everything you are reading.

Maybe the negative self talk served you when you were a child. Loo may have kept you safe as a child. This could have been the voice that said don't touch that hot stove, or look before you cross the street.

Over time, habits get developed. The voice comes on, you listen to it, and you don't question what you are being told because you have always been told how to feel or what to think. That voice is familiar and we love the familiar-even if no longer serves. The voice that just wanted to keep you safe can seep over into other parts of your life as well.

Can you see how this applies in your life? Do you hear Loo's voice? Do you listen? Take some time and really think about your list of things that Loo tells you. Do you have stories from your past that relate to your body? Do you have stories that relate to your overall self-esteem? My story about adding numbers does not relate directly with body image, however it relates directly with self-image. This story feeds the "not enough" syndrome. I have carried around the heaviness of self-hate for way too long. When I slayed the beast, I slayed this story.

When Loo wants to talk to you it's okay to acknowledge what Loo is saying. Is there anything that Loo is telling you that you need to know?

I want you to know, for absolutely sure, that you do not have to listen! Remember that you get to choose. You can be kind and gentle to Loo, and let her know that you appreciate the information, and you are not in need of her advice. You can think another thought, you can listen to another voice. The most important thing is to become aware and *conscious of your thoughts* and know that you can change them. You do not have to listen to Loo! If Loo doesn't stop, you can make a demand that Loo stop.

Think of the Supreme's song "Stop in the name of love," and sing it out loud. It is a way to shift the pattern in your brain, or scratch the record of Loo's voice.

You can invite the voice of Be-Loved, which I will tell you about later.

Isn't it time for you to shed the weight of self-hate?

When you tell your voices from the past story, you can also include stories that come from Loo, too.

Affirmation:

"I choose wisely. Each choice I make nourishes and refreshes my body, my mind, my Spirit."

Commitment:

"Today, I commit to doing my best. Each choice I make nourishes & refreshes my alignment with Spirit. (The Divine, God, Higher Power, Goddess, etc.)"

—Bernie Austin

The Beast Of Beliefs

Beliefs guide your thoughts and your thoughts create the life that you have. You are the creator of your life and each thought that you have has gotten you to where you are today. Your beliefs decide how you show up in life. Your beliefs decide how you respond and react, how you move forward or get propelled backward. This is not breaking news and most of us are somewhat comfortable with this. But have you ever thought about thoughts and beliefs that may not even be yours?

How much stuff are you carrying around that came from somewhere else and from someone else? We are programmed from childhood to absorb what is in our surroundings, including what happens in our family homes and expanding out into the world. With such easy access to world news, world events and world thoughts, we are now, more than ever carrying thoughts and beliefs from a global perspective. But the most ingrained beliefs still come from our family home.

As I was growing up, my Mom was always pregnant. I come from a family with 6 brothers and sisters, so if she wasn't always pregnant, it sure seemed like it. In those brief periods of her being not pregnant, she was hot! She had a beautiful body. I know that from looking at pictures of her. I remember she was always beautiful-pregnant or not! And I remember her dressing up in high heels and going out on weekends. I loved seeing her dressed up!

There was something else going on, though. This was something that I never thought about or can say that I consciously even noticed. My dad never thought she was thin enough. Because he didn't think she was thin enough, she didn't think she was thin enough.

There were times that he called during the day to tell her that he invited people from work to dinner that evening, and she needed to create a great meal, get the kids cleaned up for the perfunctory greeting, then hidden away. She needed to look stunning. He would criticize her in front of his friends for not being "enough." Not thin enough, smart enough-just not enough. This is not anything that I consciously witnessed, however, it was the energy in the house. I may have heard comments, but as a young girl, I didn't know what they meant.

Years later in talking with my Mom about this, she confirmed that this was indeed the case. What happened to me was I took that energy from their relationship and implanted it into my thoughts and created the belief that I was not enough. I also implanted the thought that it is really important to be thin. In fact, my worth and value come from how I look. I know that I got a lot of my beliefs about who I am and what I looked like from their relationship. So when I think about my body and how I define it, am I really defining it by what I think or by what is entangled in my parent's relationship from 50 years ago?

Here's another thought: what if your beliefs come from another lifetime? What if your beliefs come from race consciousness?

Race consciousness or race thought is the accumulated experience of the whole human race. It is a collective field of thought and belief and is a part of the subconscious mind of everyone. We are all a part of this field, and we all make decisions and form beliefs from thoughts that are not even our own.

The good news is that through self inquiry, asking questions, we can find out what beliefs we have are from our own experience or from others. And even better news is that we don't need to hold on to anything-we can change and release any beliefs that do not support the truth and beauty of who we really are.

I want you to be aware of your beliefs, and I don't think it is all that important to put a label on where each belief has come from. I want you to know that we are complicated beings made up of many thoughts and beliefs and they are not always our own. You don't need to do much more than be aware and conscious of what you are thinking and believing.

If you have you never thought about your beliefs when it comes to your body image, why not take some time now to get into your head and think about it? This is an awesome opportunity to take some time and think about what you believe and to also look at how you see things-especially your body and other people's bodies.

Remember that your belief system is what drives you, and those beliefs may not only be driven by race consciousness and family environment but also driven by some very powerful marketing and cultural myths.

Our culture tells us that beautiful equals thin, no wrinkles, no sags, lots of thick shiny hair and, recently, big lips.

If we were to believe that what we see in advertising and TV shows and movies is an accurate assessment of what's beautiful, we are all pretty much in trouble because very few people in this society meets those standards and is "really beautiful." And for some crazy reason we believe those standards to be true. Think about the absurdity of that. We buy into what the media, advertisers, and movie makers want us to think is beautiful. We take the thoughts of others and make them our own. Doesn't that piss you off? It sure makes me mad. It is time to change how we think!

What if you could create in your own mind, what beauty is? What if you could decide what is beautiful for you and only you? Would that be freeing? What if you asked the Universe to show you something beautiful today and when you looked in the mirror you saw the gift of beauty-*you*?

Imagine what it would be like to walk and talk in the world where you knew that you were beautiful just as you are right now?

What are your beliefs about beauty?

Some beliefs to question, as an example are; what do you believe about beauty? What types of people don't have a perfect body? If you have some body fat, what type of person does that make you? Is this a belief that you may want to change?

Remember that it is not important to know where all of your beliefs have come from, nor is it important to release and change each belief right now. You'd be at this for a long time! What is important, is for you to understand that you are driven by your beliefs. You can change your beliefs when you become aware and conscious of what they are. The following exercise is simply to get you used to knowing that you have the power to change your beliefs. To know that you can question what you have always thought is the opening to creating a life by design-your design-and *you* get to decide what is beautiful!

Go through the questions in this exercise and start to get a feel for where you are now.

What are your Beliefs about:

Beauty

1._____

2._____

3._____

4._____

5._____

Do these beliefs serve you?

_____

What do you want to change?

_____

_____

_____

_____

_____

What are your Beliefs about:

People who look "perfect" in the media – TV, Movies, Ads?

1._____

2._____

3._____

4._____

5._____

Do these beliefs serve you?

_____

What do you want to change?

_____

_____

_____

_____

What are your Beliefs about:

Dieting or people who diet

1._____

2._____

3._____

4._____

5._____

Do these beliefs serve you?

_____

What do you want to change?

_____

_____

_____

_____

_____

What are your Beliefs about:

Aging

1._____

2._____

3._____

4._____

5._____

Do these beliefs serve you?

_____

What do you want to change?

_____

_____

_____

_____

_____

What are your Beliefs about:

Play and Fun

1._____

2._____

3._____

4._____

5._____

Do these beliefs serve you?

_____

What do you want to change?

_____

_____

_____

_____

_____

What are your Beliefs about:

Physical activity—dancing, working out, yoga, walking etc.

1._____

2._____

3._____

4._____

5._____

Do these beliefs serve you?

_____

What do you want to change?

_____

_____

_____

_____

_____

What are your Beliefs about:

Being Worthy/Being Enough

1._____

2._____

3._____

4._____

5._____

Do these beliefs serve you?

_____

What do you want to change?

_____

_____

_____

_____

_____

Now that you are aware some of the beliefs that you have, you can change anything that doesn't serve you now.

Here is one way to deal with old beliefs that no longer serve you.

> Imagine that your beliefs are held up by the legs of the chair. Without the legs holding up the chair it would collapse.
> The legs of the chair are the supporting data that you use to hold up your beliefs. Supporting data is simply proof that comes from thoughts that you have had, and events that you have experienced or witnessed. Then you took them on to believe as true. Think of it as "I know it's true because ..."
> If you believe something to be true, you will always find data/proof to support your belief.
> Find data/proof that goes *contrary* to what you believe and the belief is changed and there is space for a new belief to be formed.
> If you want to live a life feeling good about your body, start to look for beliefs that do not support feeling good about your body. Then, find the data/proof that shows that particular belief is not valid.
> Now start to form beliefs that support feeling good about your body. Look for what is already good about your body. Look for data/proof that supports loving your body.

It looks like this:

Let's say the belief is "I need to weigh 120 pounds to feel beautiful and love my body."

Supporting data/proof that upholds that belief (the legs of the chair) could be:

> People who are on TV weigh less than that and they are considered to be beautiful.

> Clothes are made for thin people and only look good if you are really thin.
> All models are super thin.
> Only skinny people can model and models are beautiful.
> When I lose weight, people always tell me how great I look.

Now decide if any of those thoughts are worth hanging on to.

Are there any heavier people on TV that are beautiful? Think of at least two. Do you know people who weigh more than 120 pounds that you consider to be beautiful? Are there any thin people who you consider to not be beautiful?

Do you have an outfit that you feel really good in when you put it on? Do you know anyone who weighs more than 120 pounds that looks great in clothes?

Find some plus size-models on the Internet or in magazines. Are any of them beautiful?

Do you ever compliment people if they weigh more than 120 pounds?

Have you ever been complimented if you weighed more than 120 pounds and thought the person who complimented you was lying to you? (What's that about???)

Answer these questions. It helps to write down the answers so that you can see that there could be a totally different point of view about what 120 pounds means. Think of more questions that challenge this belief.

As you go through each thought about the original belief and knock out the legs, the belief starts to collapse.

Now you are almost done. You want to replace the old belief with a new belief.

You may find yourself saying, "It isn't about how much I weigh-it's about how I feel about myself. Beauty is not 120 pounds; beauty is feeling healthy, being a contribution and wearing my clothes like a super-model, and I get to define what a super model is! When I strut my stuff, I am beautiful!"

Now find supporting data that agrees with that thought.

Understanding your beliefs is a great big step towards creating loving your body now. Using the law of attraction, you can now think about the new beliefs that will guide you into self love.

_____

_____

_____

_____

_____

_____

_____

_____

_____

_____

"The more I like me, the less I want to pretend to be other people."

—Jamie Lee Curtis

Body Gratitude-30 Day Challenge

When we are feeling too fat, too thin, too young, too old, not beautiful, not loveable, hair too thin, hair too thick, it can be difficult to see what there is to be grateful for regarding our bodies. Can you list a few things off the top of your head that you are body grateful for?

By looking for things that you are grateful for each day, you automatically start seeing the beauty that is already present in yourself.

Looking for and seeing the beauty within yourself creates a shift in thinking to see the beauty in your life. This is the law of attraction in action! You begin to focus on what you have rather than what you don't. As you focus on what you have and what you love, you create more to love!

By centering your life on gratitude, you shift your thinking to what you do love about yourself and you begin to see of what's great in your life. Everything seems a little easier, a little brighter and a lot more fun!

The 30 day challenge is simple and profound. We are often grateful for things in our lives that don't relate to our bodies. Each day for 30 days, focus on body gratitude and keep a journal. Write down at least 5 things each day that you are grateful for regarding your body.

Come up with new things each day-do not repeat-dig down and *really feel the things you are grateful for.* It could be as simple as *I have arms that give great hugs.*

Get yourself:

- ➤ A journal, notebook or whatever you will enjoy writing in
- ➤ A pen that feels good to use
- ➤ A quiet space- It helps to be in the same space each day
- ➤ Open yourself to **FEELING** the feelings that come when you think about what you appreciate and are grateful for.
- ➤ Start right now and list 5 things you appreciate and are grateful for.

_____

_____

_____

_____

_____

Be-Loved

Remember Loo-Zer? Yes, I know, how can we forget? Loo is always around. I just found a new friend, and I am really excited to share her.

When I first introduced Loo in a previous book, I knew there was more to the story of Loo-Zer. I just could not figure out what it was. There is the God whisper and I knew it was along the line of that voice, but that wasn't what I was looking for. Now, a couple of years later, it came to me. Actually it came to me as I was drifting off to sleep on the night of the end of the world as we know it, December 21, 2012.

That night we drove out to the desert (Clif wanted to see the world end from there). We stayed at a place that had mineral baths. At 3:11 in the morning, the winter solstice, we were in the mineral bath with candles, and the mist of steam created a sense of wonder and possibility. It was mystical and magical. We were in the cauldron of intention, and we sat in the dark, seeing the light. The light of the stars were being held by the dark. The light of the candles were being held by the dark. Powerful things were happening, and I think it was an opening to finally hear what I have been waiting for and knowing who it is.

When I got into bed after this magical experience, I felt at peace. But I also felt a restlessness that I can't explain, and I couldn't get to sleep. The more I couldn't get to sleep, the more tense I became, because sleep is so important to me.

In most times, Loo would start in on me with "You just had this great experience and now you are laying here being all tense. You can't even do this right. Why can't you even do the simple things like just relax? Why do you even bother doing this stuff when you just blow it? You should have just stayed home like a normal person..."

This night, Loo was not present. Instead I heard a sweet voice and she had a name and her name is Be-loved, or Be. Be is my Beloved. Be is me. Be reminds me to be loved by me. Be-loved. Be has spoken to me all of my life. I don't often hear her because Loo will drown her out. For some reason that night, Loo was strangely quiet.

Be told me to simply love myself, right where I was, and to relax into that. She was kind and caring and soft and sweet. She told me that I had an amazing night and how proud she was that I was willing to go to the desert with Clif, not knowing what to do once we got there, or what would happen. It was okay to live in uncertainty. Be told me she is always there, rooting for me. Be loves it when I step into being *me* and all that I am. Be loves it when I open to new possibilities and new ways of being.

By quieting Loo, I was finally able to hear and to know that I am Beloved. You also have Be as a friend and powerful ally. Can you hear Be speak to you?

Take some time and sit quietly. You can do a formal meditation, a walking meditation, a swimming meditation or even a shower meditation. All that you need to do is drift into the land of magic, the land of quiet and peace, the place where you can hear the God whisper. The is the place where Be lives. The more you are aware and alert for Be-loved to come to you, the louder you will hear the words of encouragement, love and kindness.

Imagine what she looks like. Really use your imagination and see her with you, holding you. Is she young or older? Does she look like you? What is she wearing? Know that she is there to help you, soothe you and support you.

Be-Loved Exercise

Go inside and listen to some of the things that Be tells you on a regular basis.

Top Ten Things Be tells me:

1._____

2._____

3._____

4._____

5._____

6._____

7._____

9._____

10._____

After you have created your list of the top 10 things Be tells you, you will start to see a pattern. These will be the thoughts you will want to focus on. Once you are aware of the voice, you can keep calling her in and expand the voice of support, kindness and love.

Now you are beginning to change your thoughts!

Women Supporting Women

We have talked about the media, culture and old beliefs regarding negative self image. One of the ways we perpetuate negative self image is by passing it on and laying it onto each other. Sometimes I think women can be each other's worst enemies.

Question and please answer in truth: Do you ever look another woman up and down when she enters the room and then pass judgment on her based on her body? Remember how my family does it to each other? Do you do it to other women?

If you just did an intake of breath or got the icky feeling in your body, your answer would be yes.

I found that this is something that I used to do, and I know it came from my family's way of being. When I noticed that I did it to them and to other women, it tasted so foul to me I knew that I need to stop it.

I recently received this testimonial from a participant after she did the Love Your Body Now! Workshop. *"One of the unexpected and yet profound changes that I experienced was having shifted from a very old ingrained perspective of checking out people and labeling them. Now I look at people with the express intent of "seeing who's in there," rather than judging their body. This new outlook is amazingly refreshing and liberating. . ."*

When we sit in a circle with other women and share our stories and our pain, we find that we are all so full of not enough. Not enough in the relationship, not enough to deserve love, not enough beauty, not enough youth, not smart enough-not not not not enough of anything. Are you sometimes afraid to pick up the phone and call someone because they might not want to hear from you right now? That is being in the "not good enough" of you.

Here is something that I hear a lot. "Why is she going to your workshop? She has nothing to worry about. Look at her, she is perfect. She is thin and beautiful." And as we sit in circle and share, we find that everyone has pain and stories no matter what the outward *appearance* is. It is the same as weighing 118 pounds and thinking I was too fat. The woman who has the outer appearance of what is culturally accepted as beauty not only has to deal with her own stories, but she has to deal with how other people perceive her. The attitude of "how dare you complain about body image when you look like that" says that she doesn't get to feel bad because of her appearance. Can we please stop judging each other?

This is even deeper than body image. It goes beyond looks. Do you sometimes secretly wish that a woman you know (or maybe don't know) will fail? Maybe you wish that failure on someone else because it will make you look better. Maybe it's because you don't think she deserves it. Whatever the reason, it all goes to the "not enough" issue. Don't you think we've had enough of putting ourselves and our friends down? We all walk in shadow at times-let's become conscious of it, which is always the first step to expanding and being the love light that we are born to be.

It is my want to stand as sisters, supporting each other in being enough. What can we do to support each other? How creative can you get when it comes to helping a friend or family member to know that they are enough. Of course, it is ultimately up to them to know that truth. How about just doing it for you and modeling it? How about knowing for yourself that you are enough and in turn knowing it for other women?

The people in your life are a reflection of you. Remember the law of attraction. What energy you put out is the energy that comes back to you. If you surround yourself with catty women who love to talk about others in a negative way, you are probably putting out that energy yourself. If you want to be supported by women, then you must support women.

I am so blessed to have some of the most remarkable women in my life that I am honored to call friends. As one of my friends said so beautifully, "We are there to hold each other's dreams in our hands." We uplift and support each other when one of us is feeling down. We are there to celebrate each triumph no matter how small or how large. This has not always been the case in my life. I tell the story about the question I was asked about who would be at my funeral. At the time, I was grateful that I had a lot of brothers and sisters because they were the only ones that would show up.

Now it is a very different story. It is important for you to know that if you are not surrounded by supportive women in your life, that can change. The change begins with you. Become the woman, the Goddess that you really are and you will attract other Goddesses. It may not happen overnight, but each thing you do, each new way of being sends a message into the Universe of who you are, and the message is answered with new people coming into your life or old friends who somehow step it up a notch, to support you in who you are. Be the friend you want to have. Be the kindness you want to have. Be the love you want to have. This beautiful world is waiting for you.

May we walk in our beauty, right now, as we support and lift each other to the heights of all that is possible.

Love your body now-Lose the weight of self-hate and claim the yummy-ness of your Goddess-ness and you will be surrounded by other Goddesses who love and laugh and enrich each other's lives.

Beauty is not in the face,
Beauty is in the light of the heart.

—Kahlil Gibran

Move Your Body Now!

Get your Goddess Groove on and Dance!

Your body has an inner dance, an inner desire to express through movement. When you hear music, your body naturally moves to the rhythm. You do not have to force it or think about it. Movement is in your body. It wants to be expressed. As Kate Nash says, "Move your body's way. Your body knows and that is where your power lies."

Movement moves the flow of chi, your lifeforce. As you move you can remove blockages that keep you tight and constricted. If you have never moved your body purposefully, do it for a bit and see the release that starts to happen. By purposefully, I do not mean to do it in a measured, knowing the steps, way. I mean move it with intention and purpose of losing yourself in movement to where your mind is no longer moving your body-your inner self is moving your body.

In order to love your body, you need to feel your body. Please do this for one week. Each day, preferably in the morning, put on your favorite music. The only rule is it must be music that makes you want to move. It does not need to be any particular movment. Just start to move.

One of my favorite songs is "You can keep your hat on" by Joe Cocker. It is fun, strip teasey music and my Goddess Groove gets going with this music.

Sometimes it is fun to just put on swaying music to meditate by. Sometimes it's Tai Chi. Sometimes it's good old fashioned rock n' roll. Whatever works for you, do it.

While you are dancing, begin to feel your blood move through your body. Feel your breath. As you let your body move you, sense what that feels like. Does it feel free? Does your body want to move faster? Slower? Do you want to get down on the floor and move?

What feelings start to come up? Listen to your body. Do you judge how your body moves? Just take note and see what is there for you. Do you become more energized? Do you become tired? Do you feel sensual? Can you begin to see the Goddess emerging?

If you feel good doing this for a week, do it again for another week. Continue moving your body. As you get deeper in touch with how your body wants to move, you will get deeper in touch with who you are. You may just want to find a class that feel right for you so that you can go and dance with your sister Goddesses.

I found that dancing the Nia technique opened me up to be with other women because it is not just about movement. To find out more about Nia, go to:

http://www.nianow.com/

If you happen to be in Ventura, CA learn more at:

http://venturaniacenter.com/

Dancing is a beautiful way to love your body, right now!

Loving Your Body Now!

Imagine what it would feel like to be loved for exactly who and how you are right now.

Imagine what it would feel like to be loved and held by Spirit, God; the higher self, the presence that is within you right now.

Imagine how it would feel to have your head held, your face caressed by one who loves you unconditionally.

You have that power each and every day in each and every moment because that presence is always within you.

Take time each day to hold your hand, touch your face, your arms, your body with the love that exists in you right now.

Love Your Body Now Mirror Exercises

You have probably done mirror exercises before. Please think of this a little differently. I do not want you to think about seeing yourself differently. I want you to start to see yourself as the beauty that you already are. This is about losing the weight of self-hate.

In many mirror exercises the outcome is about changing your image. I want to shine the light on discovering the "I Am" presence that you did previously.

In the first exercise, you will be shining the light on what you don't like. In fact what you hate about your body. Shining the light brings you out of the darkness and awakens possibilities and ways of being that you haven't even thought about. Doing it in front of someone else takes the power away of those secret thoughts.

Part 1:

Go to the mirror with a partner. Looking in the mirror, give your partner an overview of how you feel about your body. Then, tell your partner and show your partner what you do not love about your body. The deeper you go and the more honest you are about the parts that you don't love or even hate, the more you will get out of this exercise. Really show the parts, grab them, shake them, squeeze them and feel the heaviness of what it means to not love yourself.

What feelings come up when you share?

***This is really, really important: For the partner that is listening–do not agree, do not react, and do not express what you think about what she is saying. You are merely a witness, giving the gift of listening.

Part 2:

When you have finished sharing the parts and things that you do not love about your body, it is time for your partner to share with you.

The partner that listened: give your partner your overview of her body. Tell her what you see. What do you love about her body? What do you love about her? When you are telling her about what you see, talk about her beauty-things that you notice that are special and unique about her. You can talk about her strong arms that give great hugs, eyes that light up, a heart that fills the room, soft skin, her sensuality and the sexy way she moves, any beauty that you see, express freely. Shower her in beauty and kind and gentle words. Most of all, be sincere and come from your heart-not your head!!

Now Switch

Thank your partner, Namaste and move off by yourself and move directly into this next exercise.

Part 1:

Becoming friends with your body—jiggle the jiggle!

This is a great exercise! It is fun and it really goes far to lift the weight of self-hate. It is time to become friends with yourself and your body. Instead of looking in the mirror and doing the "yuck" face, you can look in the mirror and wink, knowing the true Goddess that you are.

Are you ready to make peace with your body?

Put on some really fun, upbeat music.

Begin by dancing to the music. It should be music that you can't help but dance to. Once you are moving and smiling, choose a body part that you don't like. It could be your hand, foot, head, thighs, stomach-any body part and take hold of it. Rub it, scratch it, jiggle it. Get outrageous with it. Laugh with it. Joke with it. Become friends with it and smile and love it. Thank it for being a part of you

Part 2:

Sit quietly. You can put on some meditative music if you would like. Close your eyes and breathe, relaxing into the feeling of self-love. As you become calm and centered, choose a body part that you have not liked in the past. It could be your hand, foot, head, thighs, stomach-any body part. Touch that part as if you are someone who loves you just as you are, right now. Touch that part as someone who "sees" you and loves you unconditionally. Touch yourself with the caress that you imagine how God would touch you. Hold your face in your hands with the touch of the Divine. You are the Divine and you have the ability to do this anytime you want. Love your body, now!

"You can positively produce whatever you want in your body if you will fix your attention upon the Perfection of it – but do not let our attention rest upon its imperfections."

-St. Germain

Living Your Life And Loving Your Body Visualization

In order to live your life fully and love your body, you need to know what that means to you. I find that quiet meditation opens the doors to my heart's desires. Think about what your heart's desires are when it comes to your body and your life. To this point, we have talked about loving your body right now, just the way it is. Do you have a heart's desire for your body? Do you have a heart's desire for your life?

Do you want to be stronger, more flexible, to be able to hike up a mountain or swim in the ocean? If your body is not at that point just yet, love where you are right now, and give yourself the opportunity to walk into that body that can move the way you want to.

Why are you here, walking this earth? There is a reason you chose to come into this body right here and right now. Why are you here? What does your perfect day look like? How does your body move in that perfect day? What are you wearing? What is the weather like? What activities are you doing? Do you have a lot of energy? Do you take time for meditation and peaceful relaxation? Do you make love? How do you wake up-restful and ready to jump into the new day?

It is a lot of fun to get together with other women and write up your perfect day. After writing your perfect day, share your day with each other. This is so much fun and you get to know each other on an even deeper level. You can also support each other in each other's visions.

Start the process by listing what you want in your life regarding your body. Once you have some ideas about your body, expand it to what the perfect day looks like and how you move through it.

There is an actual visualization process to follow. Do you know what you want to visualize?

List some things that you can start to visualize. You can start small and gradually go big, or you can start big. Whatever you can do authentically is the best place to start!

What I want in my life regarding my body

_____

_____

_____

_____

_____

_____

_____

_____

_____

_____

_____

_____

_____

_____

_____

_____

My perfect day

_____

_____

_____

_____

_____

_____

_____

_____

_____

_____

_____

_____

_____

_____

_____

_____

_____

_____

_____

_____

_____

_____

_____

_____

_____

_____

_____

_____

_____

_____

_____

_____

_____

_____

_____

_____

_____

_____

_____

_____

This is the second-best thing that you can do for yourself every day. I hope you still remember the first one-gratitude!

Here are the simple rules for visualizing what you want, who you want to be and how you want to show up in your life.

1. Find a comfortable place to be when you vision. This could be the same place you do your gratitude journal and meditate. Doing it in the same place helps to develop a habit. Or you can do this while you are being physical. You can vision while you walk, swim, even shower.
2. Do it once a day, every day.
3. Do this practice for about 5 minutes. I like to add the visioning practice after meditation.
4. Be as detail-oriented as you can be. See the picture of yourself in your mind's eye.
5. Get into it. *Feel the feelings*. Add physical movement to really add a kick (you can do this when you are dancing or walking or swimming).
6. Visualize the end result. See yourself doing and feeling how you would be as if it already has happened. (Don't worry or think about how this is going to happen-it's not your job.)
7. Own it. Know that this is your life, even if it is unseen in this moment. Know that you are worth it and you can do it.
8. This is important-take some action out in the world to move into what you are visualizing. The Universe/Spirit is there to move things around to accommodate you, and you have to be "in the way" for miracles to happen!

It's that simple. This is a practice, so practice!

"Each of you are unique and perfect by nature's design, like a SNOWFLAKE . You are a perfect work of art. Everything about you is harmonious and balanced.

 My job is to teach you how to visually repeat that balance and perfection and bring it into your personal style."

—Amy Michelson

The Blingy Glamour Factor

Once you let your inner beauty shine out, there is no stopping the shine factor! Now that you are walking with that sway in your hips because you own the Goddess that you are, it's time for some blingy fun! Beauty does come from the inside, and there is no amount of awesome clothes, make up or shoes that will make you feel beautiful if you don't have it oozing out of you from the inside.

When you own that you are enough, that you are a magnificent creation of God and you stand in your power, then dressing up and being beautiful on the outside is awesome!

My friend, Amy Michelson is a fabulous wedding dress designer. She also does "Dress Your Essence," which means pretty much what it sounds like. She teaches you how to dress and accessorize to bring out your inner essence in the most beautiful way. Everyone has a unique way of being, right? And everyone has a unique way of dressing to bring out that being.

She taught me about my colors, what type of neckline is best for me, what style of clothes to wear for different occasions-even how to dress up the everyday schlepping look. A belt or a piece of jewelry can make all of the difference! Things I never even thought about. There is no reason to walk around feeling and looking schleppy. (I think you know what that means!) If you are shining on the inside, maybe you want a little bling on the outside. There is nothing wrong with this–in fact, it's a good thing. The only thing to be careful of is sliding back to thinking a shiny bracelet will give you value. *You give you value.* The bracelet mirrors back your bling from inside. And that is a lot of fun!

Amy asks *"Have you ever found yourself looking in a department store mirror thinking..."If only I were skinnier, taller, had bigger boobs, a smaller butt...THEN this dress would look good on me?"*

And her answer is *"YOU are PERFECT exactly as you are. There is nothing wrong with YOU there is something wrong with the outfit you have on. What's wrong is the outfit you have on doesn't live up to your unique beauty, not the other way around!"*

How freeing and cool is that? Instead of looking at our bodies as being wrong, we can look at the clothes being wrong for our bodies. No one ever taught me this and it has changed how I think about clothes and shopping.

I am not going to teach you how to do what Amy does here because only Amy can do that. I want to put this into your consciousness the next time you go shopping. Look for clothes that speak to you, not what the latest trend is. When you put on the "right" outfit, you know it.

I do want to make sure that you get that I am not saying not get dressed up, and I am not saying that you shouldn't wear makeup. Do it for fun. Don't do it because you think others will like you better if you do. Know that you are already perfect AND we are in these human bodies, so let's have some fun with them!

This same idea applies to what you eat and how you move your body. When you embrace the value of your existence, just because you exist, and you know the beauty that you are, you will want your temporary home, your body to be healthy and you will want to be able to move with ease.

When I was a realtor and lived in a small town in Colorado, I would never go out of my house without makeup on and looking good. Actually, that had been true for my life ever since I was in seventh grade and started wearing makeup. No one ever saw me without makeup and my hair done. I was so insecure with how I looked because I thought how I looked was my value. I always looked put together. I was afraid no one would like me if they knew how I really looked, but I didn't know that's what was going on.

About 7 years ago, I went to a weekend workshop. It was a women's weekend about healing and empowerment. Before going, I received a registration package, and in that package I was asked to come without jewelry or makeup. This was a weekend for going deep within, and it was not about going to impress anyone. This was not a casual request—they wanted me to sign a commitment that I would not wear jewelry or makeup. I signed it and sent it back.

Of course, I showed up with jewelry and makeup. I didn't think that anyone would really care or notice. They had this thing they called *accountability* on the very first night. Accountability is all about being accountable for what you say you would do. When I was challenged on the jewelry and makeup, I was able to express my fear about not being liked if people could see what I really looked like. I really believed that people would like me, if I looked good and they would not like me, if I did not. This was the first time I really saw it in those terms.

Throughout the weekend there were many insights and tears. At one point in my most vulnerable and blubbering moments, one of the staff came up to me. He told me that in that moment I was truly beautiful because I was being authentic and real. He said he saw the inner beauty in me, and that was life-changing for me. No one had ever said anything like that to me, and I was open to hearing it when he said it.

For a while after that, I didn't want to wear makeup-that lasted a little while, and then I got that it can be fun if I am not using it to make myself likeable or worthy. It is just fun to accentuate my eyes and of course I want to look good. But it comes from an inside state, rather than an outside state. Do you get the difference?

Please understand that this whole love your body now stuff is not about *not* wanting to be in shape, eat well and dress with style. It is all about why you do it and how you feel about yourself in your skin. It is a fine distinction, and it is huge. Your beauty shines from the inside out. Let it shine!

Goddess Groove

Are you ready to "Lose the weight of self-hate and gain the yummy-ness of Goddess-ness?" Are you ready to get your "Goddess Groove" on? Here is a recap of what that means.

"When I think about getting my Goddess Groove on, I think about owning the fact that I am beautiful and sexy. Goddess Groove is all about redefining what we believe about our bodies, and knowing who we are. It is about **not** buying into what marketing and the media, our culture or others have told us to believe is beautiful."

"Goddess Groove is the celebration of female sensuality and femininity. It is all about embracing and loving your beauty, both inner and outer beauty, and celebrating the female form in all shapes, sizes and colors."

"Your Goddess Groove is simply knowing your own God-ness and coming from that place in everything you do."

"Getting your Goddess Groove on opens the door to creating new relationships with others who have their Goddess Groove on!"

"Getting your Goddess Groove on is about owning and being responsible for your life and how you see yourself. Your Goddess Groove is about claiming your own Divinity—your phenomenalness!"

"Getting your Goddess Groove on is about joy and laughter. It is about lightening up and knowing that you are so much more than the jiggle. The scars tell a story. The wrinkles tell a story. You are a wonder simply because you are here. Love the moment, love yourself and love your body."

"Getting your Goddess Groove on is about being kind to yourself. Your inner Goddess wants you to treat yourself like you would treat your best friend. It is not about punishing yourself with physical exercise for the sake of losing weight. It is not about lifting weights and suffering. And there is nothing wrong with lifting weights or going out for a run! It is about doing what feels good and is joyful. It is all about movement and self-expression. It is about being in your body and enjoying all of the things your body can do! What type of movement feels amazing and fun to you? Do that!"

"Getting your Goddess Groove on is about moving forward and using what you have learned to help not only yourself but others. How can you influence someone else by having walked through your pain and into your Goddess?"

"Getting your Goddess Groove on means that you define what is beautiful. Your beauty is defined by you. You are beautiful."

"Getting your Goddess Groove on means not wasting any of the juiciness of life on not being enough! So get over it already and get *your Goddess Groove On!*"

"Getting your Goddess Groove on is about asking empowering questions that delight."

"Get your Goddess Groove on and dance! Your body has an inner dance, an inner desire to express through movement. When you hear music your body naturally moves to the rhythm. You do not have to force it or think about it. Movement is in your body. It wants to be expressed."

"Get your Goddess Groove on and decide who you want to be."

"Become the woman, the Goddess that you really are and you will attract other Goddesses. It may not happen overnight, but each thing you do, each new way of being sends a message into the Universe of who you are, and the message is answered with new people coming into your life or old friends who somehow step it up a notch to support you in who you are. Be the friend you want to have. Be the kindness you want to have. Be the love you want to have. This beautiful world is waiting for you."

"Getting your yummy Goddess Groove on is all about being juicy, passionate and vulnerable. Then, coming from this place, giving your gift."

"Love your body now-Get over it and get your Goddess Groove on and you will be surrounded by other Goddesses who love and laugh and enrich each other's lives."

"The idea of women as goddesses helps us along, because goddesses are powerful, beautiful forces of nature. They embrace and own all aspects of self and they do not apologize for who they are or what they do."

—Laurie Sue Brockway

I Vow

At this point I hope you are with me in knowing that it is time to lose the heaviness of self-hate and slay the beast of negative self-image. If you have done the exercises and have thought about where your thoughts come from, it is time to take the vow!

Please remember that this is not gospel. If it resonates in your body and you feel this is your truth, then make the vow. If you do not agree with something, change it so that it is true for you. You are in control of your thoughts and feelings when it comes to your body and your mind. No one else can tell you what is right or wrong or good or bad. In fact there is no right or wrong or good or bad. Your truth may ring differently than mine. There is no judgment.

Maybe you have walked through the portal of having a direct experience of the Truth. Maybe you love your body right now, just as it is. Take some time and reflect on the vows below. I do not take this lightly and I am asking you to not take it lightly. Print this out and tape it to your mirror so that you can remember your truth.

I VOW TO SLAY THE BEAST OF NEGATIVE SELF-IMAGE

I know that to love and respect myself, the Divine and Infinite Being that I am, I must love and respect my body. With that thought in mind, I VOW to do the following:

I VOW to stand proud and celebrate knowing that my body is a vessel that holds the essence of who I really am.

I VOW to think different thoughts when it comes to my body. To think of all of the different ways my body supports and carries me through my daily life. To think of how my arms can hug, how my legs carry me to help others or to dance in the rain. To think of how my smile can change someone else's life and of how my touch comforts.

I VOW to remember that I am worthy just as I am. No one else defines my worth – I define my worth and I know that I am worthy because I AM.

I VOW to look for the beauty in everyone. I will stop judging others and comparing myself to others. I compliment myself and others often.

I VOW to remember that my life is filled with infinite possibilities and blessings.

I VOW to honor my body and keep it well hydrated and well nourished. To keep it rested, flexible and strong.

I VOW to live today and do all of the things that bring me joy. I will not wait until I have a better or different body. I will swim, dance, walk, hike, and make love with abandon.

I VOW to not waste another moment of time disrespecting myself and worrying about fat, cellulite, pimples, rolls or any other perceived body problem.

I VOW to know and to remember that my weight or my age do not define who I am.

I VOW to discover my own Goddess Groove and get it on!

I VOW to love myself and my body RIGHT NOW. Not when I lose weight, have a better haircut, can fit into those jeans, have bigger breasts (or smaller) or when my complexion clears up. I love myself NOW!

Thank you for coming on this quest with me — the quest to find your Goddess Groove and to own the Goddess that is within you.

Know that you are loved, that you are perfect and that you get to choose, in each and every moment, how to feel. You get to choose what is beautiful. You get to choose how you want to live your life. How do *you* want to live your life?

I choose living with love and with passion. I choose to dance and to shimmer. I choose to love my body, right now! What do you choose? I would love to hear from you about your journey and what you choose!

Good bye for now, with love and blessings,

Maria

IMAGINE A RETREAT CREATED JUST FOR YOU

➢ Imagine time in a beautiful place, surrounded by nature.

➢ Imagine breaking through your self-love barriers.

➢ Imagine having time finding out what is keeping you blocked from being everything you want.

➢ Imagine creating a deep connection with other women, supporting each other in sacred space as you share your inner most struggles and deep longings.

➢ Imagine having time becoming clear about who you are.

➢ Imagine having uninterrupted time away from it all: no computer, no phone.

➢ Imagine having time just for you.

➢ Imagine having time to learn and to know who you Really are.

➢ Imagine having time to dance, and then dance some more!

IMAGINE having time to
IMAGINE

If this sounds good, keep
on imagining...And then do
it!

Love Your Body Now!

Retreat or Vision Quest

Call or write to Maria for more information and to schedule your
time to immerse in Loving Your Body Now!

Maria@MariaBucaro.com

www.MariaBucaro.com

About Maria Bucaro

Maria is a guide who inspires and empowers you in living purposefully and powerfully. She is a unique speaker that all women can relate to because she is authentic and real. Her message comes straight from her heart and penetrates the soul.

Maria teaches from real-life experience, using the same principles that transformed her past pain and struggle into a life of inspiration, purpose, and success.

Maria realized that a balanced life equals a life of love and happiness. This includes feeling good about the body. A negative body image keeps us from living a life of joy and freedom.

She began studying and integrating the great spiritual teachings as well and became a Wilderness Guide, leading vision quests.

Maria has put together her accumulated wisdom and is inspired to share and guide you in releasing the old and limiting beliefs and embracing who you REALLY are. Maria's life work awakens you to knowing that you create the life you have and you have the power to choose from infinite possibility.

She enjoys creating sacred space, being in nature, reading, dancing, and especially building community.

Maria's Purpose: *"The purpose of my life is to shimmer and to radiate love to those around me through my dance of life"*

Maria lives her purpose by:

Living BIG and releasing small thoughts and ideas. This inspires and empowers people to awaken to their own creative power and Divine presence and an inner knowing of their own greatness.

Living without regret-jumping into any situation with love and abandon! Her example helps to guide people to transcend fear, limiting beliefs, distorted perceptions of their body and self worth.

Living with kindness. Not just with those around her, but with herself as well. Living with kindness is living with love!

Maria Bucaro-Please Join Us!

Maria leads vision quests, facilitates and guides workshops and retreats and loves connecting one-on-one.

Maria is available to come to your area if you have a group that is ready to go and grow in consciousness!

Maria is available for speaking engagements and would love to come and speak to your group.

You can find more about Maria at:

www.MariaBucaro.com

Contact Maria at:

Maria@MariaBucaro.com

19469511R00106

Made in the USA
Charleston, SC
25 May 2013